AIRCRAFT ARCHIVE

VOLUME 1
POST-WAR JETS

Contents

A DETAILED COLLECTION OF ORIGINAL SCALE AIRCRAFT DRAWINGS

Introduction

Since the earliest days of the Wright Brothers and the pioneers of European aviation, the ever-changing shape of the aeroplane has always held a special fascination. At first, the basic distinction of canard, tractor, pusher monoplane or biplane conveyed an adequate identity of the design. However, sketches soon began to appear in the magazines which reported aerial races and the latest developments were eagerly sought by enthusiasts, among them model makers and even competitive designers.

So began a practice which became a major feature among aeronautical publications and one which this series of *Aircraft Archive* sets out to preserve in collective form. What follows is a selection from the files of 'Aeromodeller' and 'Scale Models', two of the many monthly magazines from the original Model Aeronautical Press, now part of Argus Specialist Publications.

The books in this series form a representative group of subjects. Each is a typical example of skill and dedication applied by an amateur researcher over countless hours of translating measurements and photographic interpretation into a multiple-view scale drawing which, in fact, no manufacturer could ever provide! For it may come as a surprise, but the reality is that manufacturers' general arrangement drawings have little value in the factories, are rarely accurate in shape or scale and, without exception, illustrate the aeroplane in a stage long since superseded by production variants. It is the sub-assembly, or component detail drawing, which offers priceless data for the researcher to complete the jigsaw puzzle of any aeroplane. That is, of course, if such drawings become available as many of the records are now destroyed.

Access to the real thing is the ideal but how can one measure each panel, check every angle and record all the shapes? It takes a special sort of dedication to undertake such a mammoth task. A museum visit will confirm the enormity of the undertaking. Aeroplanes are almost always bigger than imagined. The tape measure becomes inadequate when required to confirm distances between extremities that are intercepted by protrusions, and the draughtsman resorts to that original method of projecting chalk marks on the floor. In this way, the preparation of a drawing reverses early procedures when designs were actually created out of chalked plans on the factory concrete!

Similarly, half a century of progress later, the three-view draughtsman can reflect with pride on the compliment that some of the museum restorations could only be completed to such fine standards through the part his work had played in the re-build.

Flattery comes in oblique forms. A priority requisite for film and documentary makers has been reference to the only general arrangement available, perpetuated for modellers and aero enthusiasts through plan services. The engineering director of a major airport has used these drawings to plan a new maintenance hangar. A restorer, on his acquisition of a foreign airframe, was able to complete his job and satisfy inspectorates through the research documentation borrowed from a three-view draughtsman, and that world famous *Magnificent Men in their Flying Machines* film depended to a considerable extent on those early sketches.

The modelling world owes another debt to the three-view draughtsman. True scale models, whether in moulded plastic or from such sophisticated composites as large radio controlled flying replicas, have emerged in vast numbers from kit boxes or individual designs, all based upon the initial researchers who produced a frozen view of the whole aeroplane.

Demand for accuracy and authenticity originated through the work of James Hay Stevens in 'Aeromodeller'. He was among the first to adopt 1/72nd scale, based on the Imperial measure of one sixth of an inch representing one foot. Opening standards, as set by James Stevens, were taken up through the series of *Aircraft of the Fighting Powers* volumes published by Harborough, an associated company. Wartime urgency quickly generated a new breed of detail draughtsman, typified by Harry

◀ George Cox contemplates the intricacies of the main undercarriage gear of a Republic F-84F Thunderstreak 'on loan' from the US Air Force.

Cooper and Owen Thetford. After seven volumes and the creation of an *Aircraft Described* series, centred on civil aircraft by Eddie Riding, 1/72nd scale was firmly established, and the fine detail in the drawings reached levels of intricacy to satisfy the most demanding enthusiast – though not for long!

From the immediate postwar years to the present day, the levels of minutiae have soared far beyond the first conceptions. Out of *Aircraft Described* came *Aeroplanes in Outline* and *Famous Biplanes* and, through forty years of publication in 'Aeromodeller' magazine, a band of skilled contributors built up a series which now comes in book form.

The drawings reflect the individual character of the originator. Each was in its time a labour of love, the fruits of which have been the immense pleasure given to students, collectors and aeromodellers. If, by reproduction in this form we commemorate their work permanently, rather than in a transient monthly magazine, then we will have rewarded both the draughtsmen and the reader with a treasure store.

◀ Pat Lloyd, tape measure in hand, about to get to grips with a Stampe biplane.

De Havilland Venom FB Mks 1 and 4

Country of origin: Great Britain.
Type: Single-seat, land-based fighter-bomber.
Dimensions: Wing span 41ft 8in *12.70m*; length 31ft 10in *9.70m*; height (FB Mk 1) 7ft 4in *2.23m*, (FB Mk 4) 6ft 10½in *2.10m*; wing area 282 sq ft *26.2m²*.

Weights: Empty 8926lb *4050kg*; loaded 15,400lb *6987kg*.
Powerplant: One de Havilland Ghost 103 turbojet of 4850lb *2200kg* static thrust.
Performance: Maximum speed 640mph *1030kph* at sea level; initial climb rate about 4330ft/min *1320m/min*; service

ceiling about 39,500ft *12,000m*.
Armament: Four fixed 20mm Hispano cannon, plus (optional) up to 2000lb *907kg* of external ordnance.
Service: First flight (FB Mk 1) 2 September 1949.

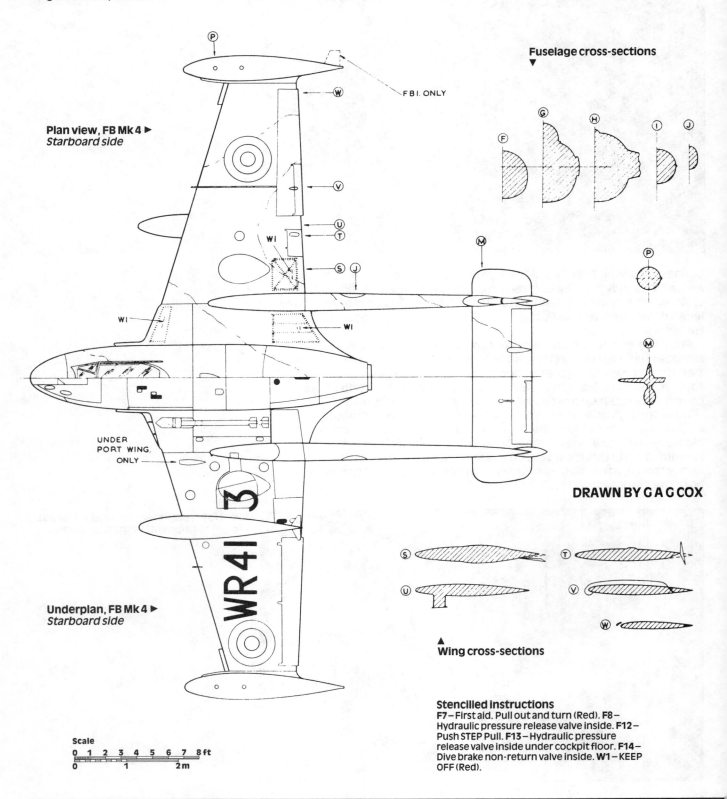

Plan view, FB Mk 4 ▶
Starboard side

F B I. ONLY

Fuselage cross-sections ▼

UNDER PORT WING. ONLY

DRAWN BY G A G COX

Underplan, FB Mk 4 ▶
Starboard side

▲ **Wing cross-sections**

Scale
0 1 2 3 4 5 6 7 8 ft
0   1   2 m

Stencilled instructions
F7 – First aid. Pull out and turn (Red). **F8** – Hydraulic pressure release valve inside. **F12** – Push STEP Pull. **F13** – Hydraulic pressure release valve inside under cockpit floor. **F14** – Dive brake non-return valve inside. **W1** – KEEP OFF (Red).

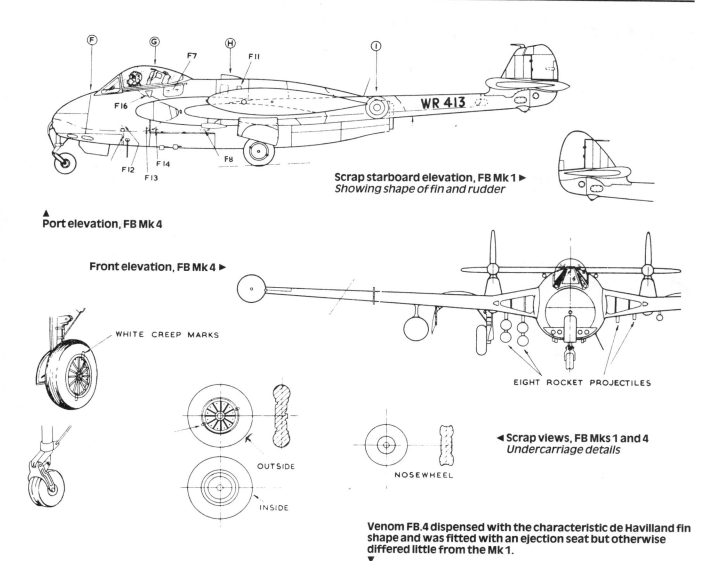

F G H I

F7 F11

F16

F12 F13 F14 F8

WR 413

Scrap starboard elevation, FB Mk 1 ▶
Showing shape of fin and rudder

▲
Port elevation, FB Mk 4

Front elevation, FB Mk 4 ▶

WHITE CREEP MARKS

OUTSIDE

INSIDE

NOSEWHEEL

EIGHT ROCKET PROJECTILES

◄ Scrap views, FB Mks 1 and 4
Undercarriage details

Venom FB.4 dispensed with the characteristic de Havilland fin shape and was fitted with an ejection seat but otherwise differed little from the Mk 1.
▼

Lockheed F-94C Starfire

Country of origin: USA.
Type: Two-seat, land-based, all-weather fighter.
Dimensions: Wing span 37ft 4in *11.38m*; length 44ft 6in *13.56m*; height 14ft 11in *4.55m*; wing area 238 sq ft *22.11m²*.
Weights: Empty 13,450lb *6103kg*;

maximum loaded 24,200lb *10,980kg*.
Powerplant: One Pratt & Whitney J48-P-5 centrifugal, afterburning tubojet of 6250lb *2835kg* static thrust.
Performance: Maximum speed 646mph *1040kph*; initial climb rate 7980ft/min *2430m/min*; service ceiling 48,000ft

14,630m; range (maximum) 1250 miles *2010km*.
Armament: Forty-eight 2.75in *70mm* 'Mighty Mouse' rockets in nose and wing pods.
Service: First flight 19 January 1950.

Port elevation, F-94C
▼

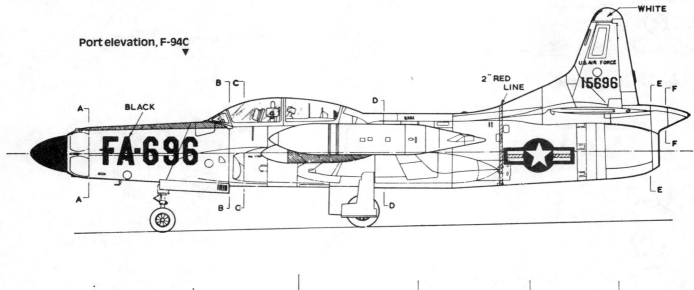

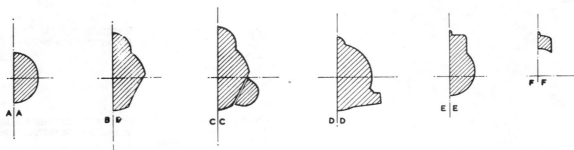

▲
Fuselage cross-sections

Each of the F-94C's wing-tip pods held a dozen air-to-air rockets, complementing the two dozen packed in the nose.
▼

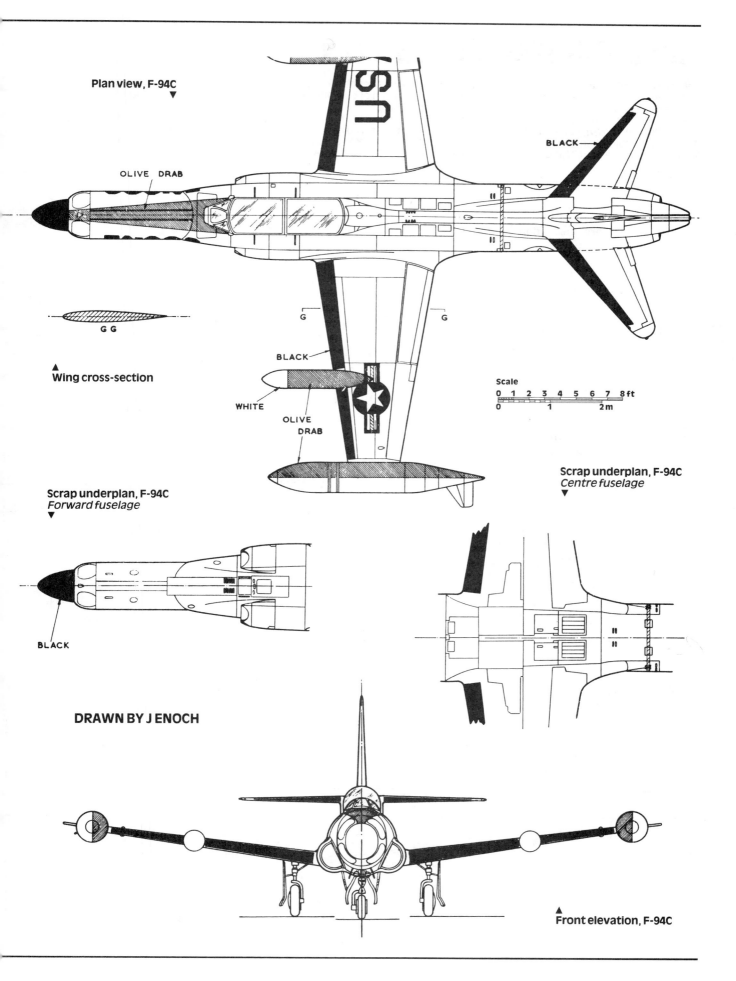

Plan view, F-94C
▼

BLACK →

OLIVE DRAB

G G

Wing cross-section
▲

BLACK

WHITE

OLIVE DRAB

Scale
0 1 2 3 4 5 6 7 8 ft
0   1   2 m

Scrap underplan, F-94C
Centre fuselage
▼

Scrap underplan, F-94C
Forward fuselage
▼

BLACK

DRAWN BY J ENOCH

Front elevation, F-94C
▲

Avro CF-100 Canada Mk 4

Country of origin: Canada.
Type: Two-seat, land-based, long-range, all-weather fighter.
Dimensions: Wing span 53ft 7in *16.33m*; length 54ft 2in *16.51m*; height 15ft 6½in *4.74m*; wing area 540 sq ft *50.16m²*.
Weights: Loaded about 37,000lb *16,800kg*.

Powerplant: Two Orenda Mk 11 axial-flow turbojets each of over 7000lb *3180kg* static thrust.
Performance: Maximum speed (dive) over Mach 1; initial climb rate over 12,000ft/min *3660m/min*; service ceiling over 45,000ft *13,700m*; range over 1150 miles *1850km*.

Armament: Eight fixed 0.5in machine guns in belly pack, plus 60 rockets in wing-tip pods.
Service: First flight (prototype) 19 January 1950, (Mk 4) 11 October 1952; service entry (Mk 4) early 1954.

Front elevation
▼

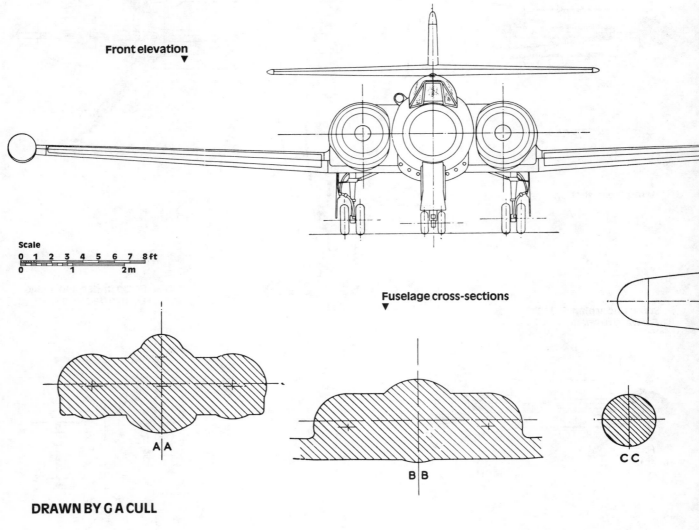

Scale
0 1 2 3 4 5 6 7 8 ft
0   1   2 m

Fuselage cross-sections
▼

A|A

B|B

C C

DRAWN BY G A CULL

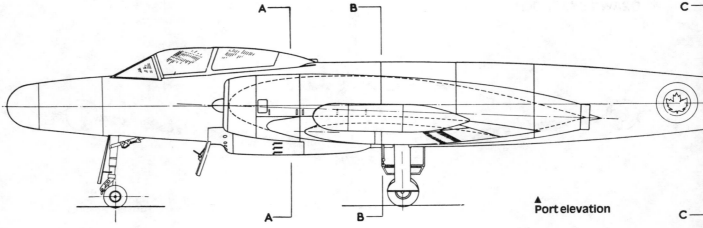

A   B   C

A   B

▲ Port elevation

C

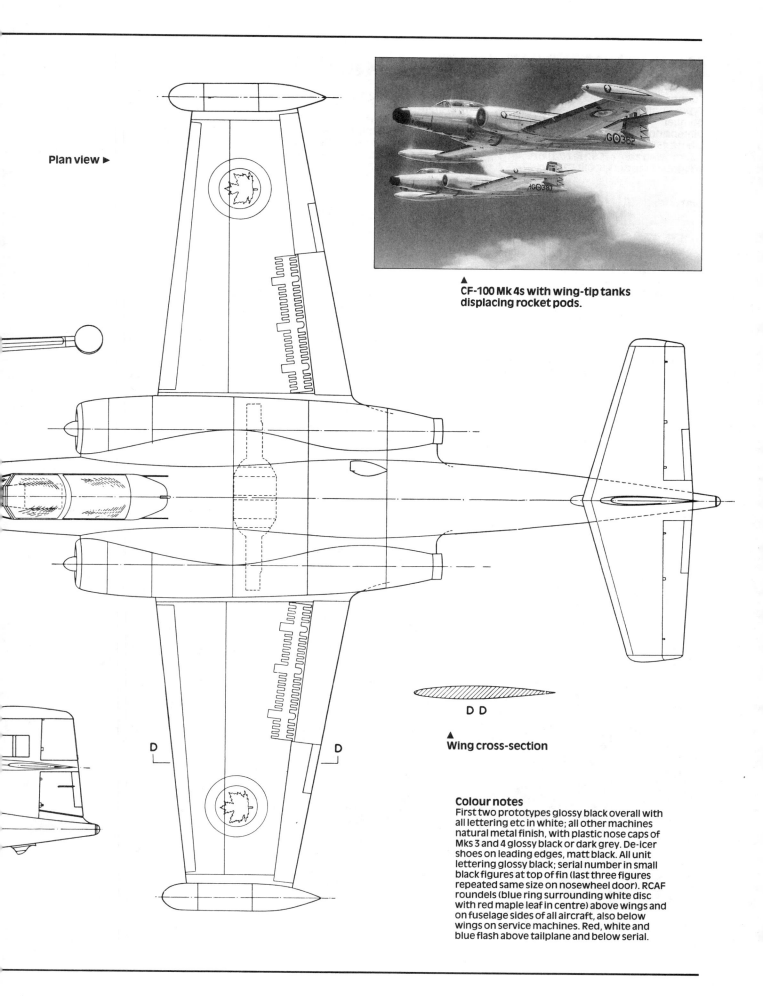

Plan view ▶

▲
CF-100 Mk 4s with wing-tip tanks displacing rocket pods.

D D

▲
Wing cross-section

Colour notes
First two prototypes glossy black overall with all lettering etc in white; all other machines natural metal finish, with plastic nose caps of Mks 3 and 4 glossy black or dark grey. De-icer shoes on leading edges, matt black. All unit lettering glossy black; serial number in small black figures at top of fin (last three figures repeated same size on nosewheel door). RCAF roundels (blue ring surrounding white disc with red maple leaf in centre) above wings and on fuselage sides of all aircraft, also below wings on service machines. Red, white and blue flash above tailplane and below serial.

Republic F-84F Thunderstreak

Country of origin: USA.
Type: Single-seat, land-based fighter-bomber.
Dimensions: Wing span 33ft 6in *10.21m*; length 43ft 4in *13.21m*; height 14ft 4in *4.37m*; wing area 325 sq ft *30.19m²*.
Weights: Empty 13,800lb *6261kg*;

maximum 28,000lb *12,700kg*.
Powerplant: One Wright J65-3 turbojet of 7220lb *3276kg* thrust.
Performance: Maximum speed 695mph *1120kph*; initial climb rate 8200ft/min *2500m/min*; service ceiling 46,000ft *14,000m*; range (clean) over 850 miles

1350km.
Armament: Six fixed 0.5in Colt-Browning machine guns and (optional) up to 6000lb *2720kg* of ordnance.
Service: First flight (prototype) 14 February 1951; service entry 3 December 1952.

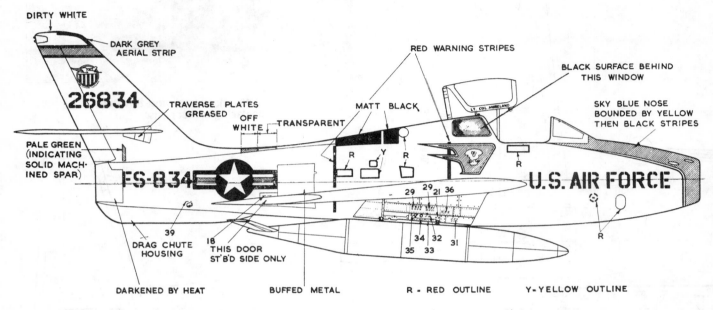

Starboard elevation, F-84F-45-RE

Close-in view of the 'Streak's nose shows complex undercarriage gear and cannon ports above intake.

▲ Port side view of 91st FBS F-84F depicted in the drawings in this plan set.

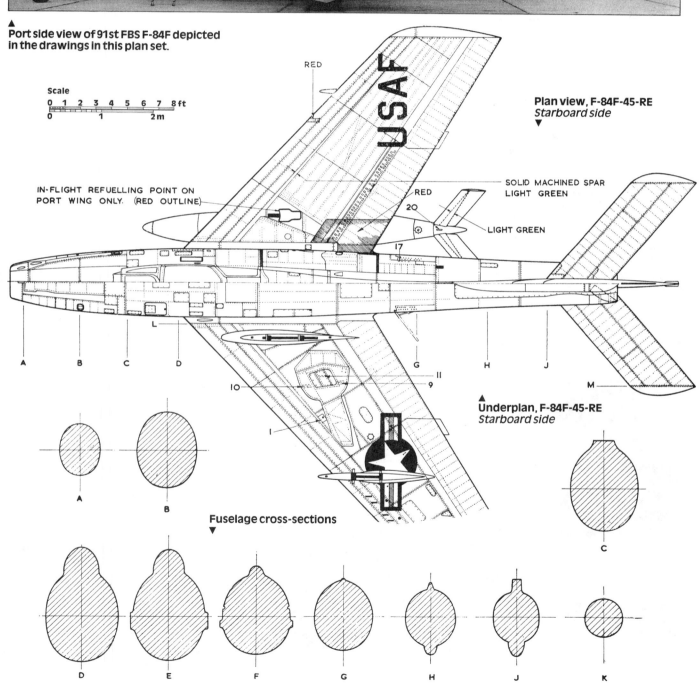

Scale
0 1 2 3 4 5 6 7 8 ft
0   1   2m

RED

USAF

IN-FLIGHT REFUELLING POINT ON
PORT WING ONLY. (RED OUTLINE)

Plan view, F-84F-45-RE
Starboard side
▼

SOLID MACHINED SPAR
LIGHT GREEN

RED

20

LIGHT GREEN

17

A   B   C   D

L

G   H   J

11

10   9

M

1

▲ **Underplan, F-84F-45-RE**
Starboard side

A   B   C

Fuselage cross-sections
▼

D   E   F   G   H   J   K

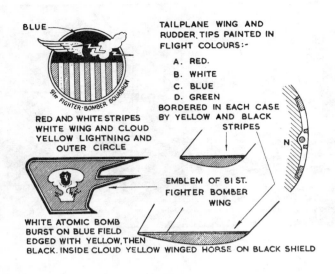

BLUE

9th FIGHTER·BOMBER SQUADRON

RED AND WHITE STRIPES
WHITE WING AND CLOUD
YELLOW LIGHTNING AND
OUTER CIRCLE

WHITE ATOMIC BOMB
BURST ON BLUE FIELD
EDGED WITH YELLOW, THEN
BLACK. INSIDE CLOUD YELLOW WINGED HORSE ON BLACK SHIELD

TAILPLANE WING AND
RUDDER TIPS PAINTED IN
FLIGHT COLOURS:-

A. RED.
B. WHITE
C. BLUE
D. GREEN
BORDERED IN EACH CASE
BY YELLOW AND BLACK
STRIPES

EMBLEM OF 81 ST.
FIGHTER BOMBER
WING

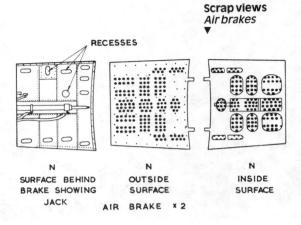

Scrap views
Air brakes
▼

RECESSES

N
SURFACE BEHIND
BRAKE SHOWING
JACK

N
OUTSIDE
SURFACE

AIR BRAKE × 2

N
INSIDE
SURFACE

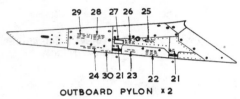

29 28 27 26 25

24 30 21 23   22   21

OUTBOARD PYLON × 2

▲
Scrap views, F-84F-45-RE
*Details of markings applied to 52-6834,
91st FBS, 81st FBW*

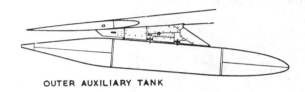

OUTER AUXILIARY TANK

▲
Scrap starboard elevation

Aircraft 52-7102 with canopy raised. Fairing beneath tail pipe
houses drag 'chute.
▼

Front elevation, F-84F-45-RE
▼

Wing and tailplane cross-sections
▼

L

M

YELLOW
INSIDE
SURFACE

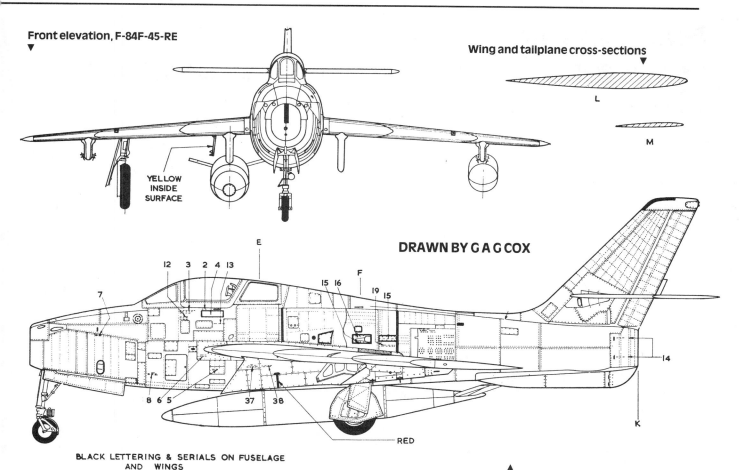

E

12 3 2 4 13

F

15 16

19 15

7

14

8 6 5

37 38

K

RED

DRAWN BY G A G COX

BLACK LETTERING & SERIALS ON FUSELAGE
AND WINGS

▲
Port elevation, F-84F-45-RE

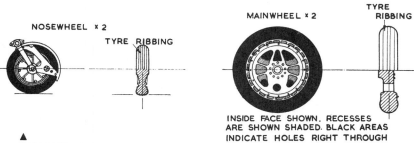

NOSEWHEEL × 2

TYRE RIBBING

MAINWHEEL × 2

TYRE
RIBBING

INSIDE FACE SHOWN. RECESSES
ARE SHOWN SHADED. BLACK AREAS
INDICATE HOLES RIGHT THROUGH

▲
Scrap views
Undercarriage details

NOSEWHEEL AND MAINWHEEL ASSEMBLIES
SIMPLIFIED

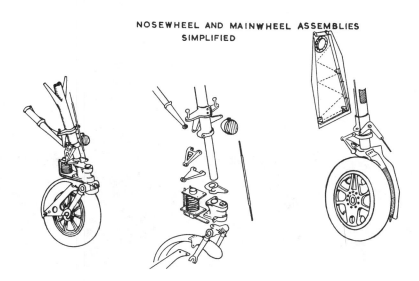

Stencilled instructions
1. External power receptacle 24 volts. 2. No step. 3. US Air Force model F84F-45RE. AF Serial No 52-6681A. Project No AFE F-477. 4. Warning. This aircraft contains a seat ejection and canopy jettison initiators containing explosive charges. See TO for complete instructions. 5. Duct screen clear out. 6. Attach wing cover here. 7. Attach nose cover here. 8. Caution. Stand clear when venting pneumatic system. 9. To open unlock camlocks and remove 3 screws. 10. To open unlock 3 camlocks and remove 1 screw. 11. For jack point. 12. (Detailed fuelling instructions). 13. Alieron booster control. 14. Tail cover slot. 15. Fire ingress door. 16. Spark plug access. 17. Tail pipe clamps. 18. Seat pins. 19. Battery location aft of nosewheel door. 20. No lift. 21. Sway brace. 22. Torque sway brace stems etc. 23. Bomb rack inspection holes. 24. Deflate cyls before removal of tank or pylon. 25. Release manual lever 52A rack. 26. Caution torque and pylon attaching bolts 71–80 ft lbs. 27. Caution. Explosive squibs inside. 28. Fill aft gauge to center of green arc on dial after pylon is installed on wing. 29. Fill fwd gauge to center of green arc on dial after pylon is installed on wing. 30. Tank elect plug. 31. Remove fairing and frag rack door when flying chemical tank and install 37W/9038-1. 32. For wind up bomb hoisting. 33. Tighten sway brace stems finger tight after tank is fueled. 34. Bomb rack inspection holes. 35. Release manual lever 52A rack. 36. Caution. Torque and pylon attaching bolts 100–110 ft lbs. 37. Caution. Disconnect manual controls and electrical harness before moving pylon. 38. Install all electrical connections with key way fwd. 39. Fuel vent.

Boulton Paul P.111A

Country of origin: Great Britain
Type: Single-seat, land-based research aircraft.
Dimensions: Wing span 33ft 5½in *10.20m*; length 26ft 1in *7.95m*; height 12ft 6½in *3.82m*.
Weights: No data available.
Powerplant: One Rolls-Royce Nene centrifugal-flow turbojet of 5000lb *2268kg* thrust.
Performance: No data available.
Armament: None.
Service: First flight (P.111) 10 October 1951, (P.111A) 2 July 1953.

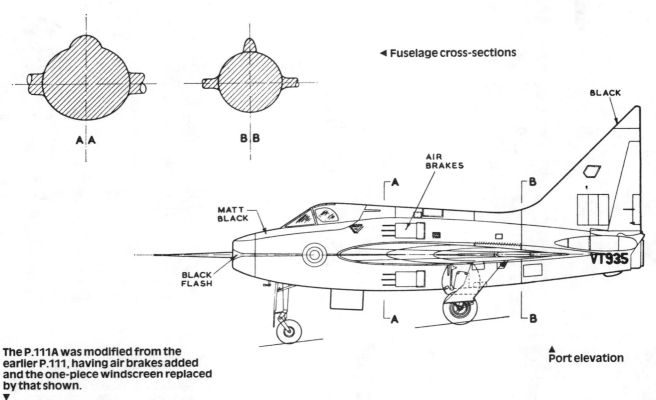

◀ Fuselage cross-sections

A A

B B

BLACK

AIR BRAKES

MATT BLACK

BLACK FLASH

VT935

▲ Port elevation

The P.111A was modified from the earlier P.111, having air brakes added and the one-piece windscreen replaced by that shown.
▼

VT935

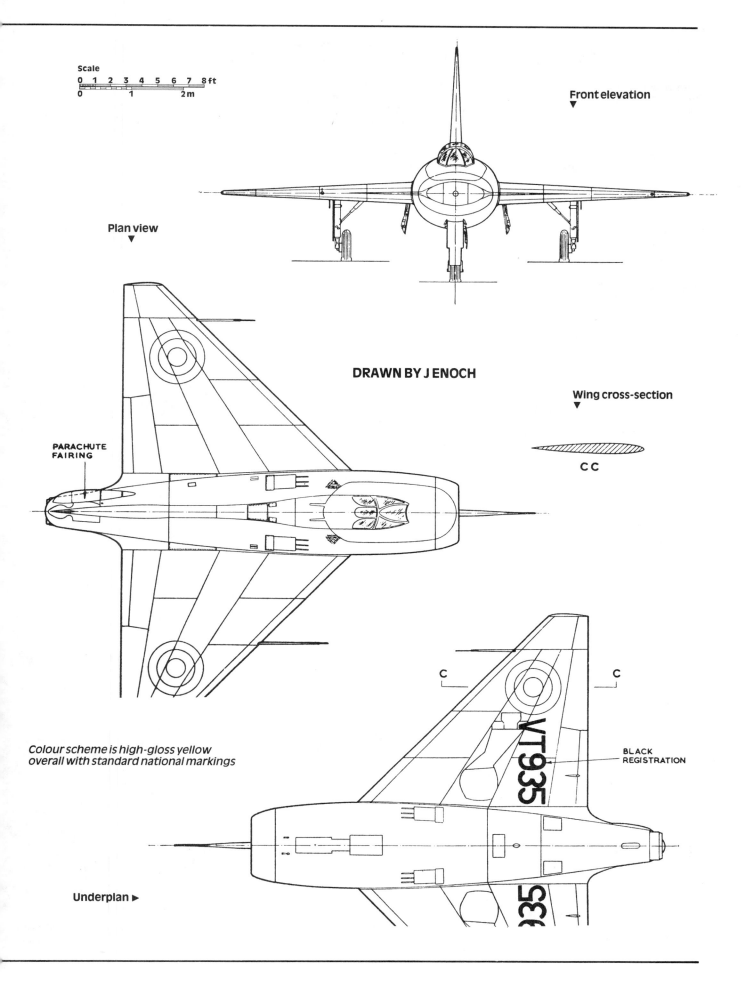

Scale

0 1 2 3 4 5 6 7 8 ft

0   1   2 m

Front elevation
▼

Plan view
▼

DRAWN BY J ENOCH

Wing cross-section
▼

C C

PARACHUTE
FAIRING

*Colour scheme is high-gloss yellow
overall with standard national markings*

C   C

VT935

BLACK
REGISTRATION

Underplan ▶

North American F-100D Super Sabre

Country of origin: USA.
Type: Single-seat, land-based fighter-bomber.
Dimensions: Wing span 38ft 9½in *11.82m*; length (exc probe) 49ft 6in *15.09m*; height 16ft 2¾in *4.95m*; wing area 385 sq ft *35.76m²*.
Weights: Empty 21,000lb *9528kg*;

maximum loaded 34,832lb *15,804kg*.
Powerplant: One Pratt & Whitney J57-21A two-shaft, afterburning turbojet of 16,950lb *7690kg* maximum thrust.
Performance: Maximum speed 865mph *1390kph* (Mach 1.3) at altitude; initial climb rate (clean) 16,000ft/min *4875m/min*; service ceiling about 45,000ft

13,700m; range (external fuel) about 1500 miles *2415km*.
Armament: Four fixed 20mm M39E cannon, plus (optional) up to 7500lb *3400kg* of external ordnance.
Service: First flight (YF-100A) 25 May 1953.

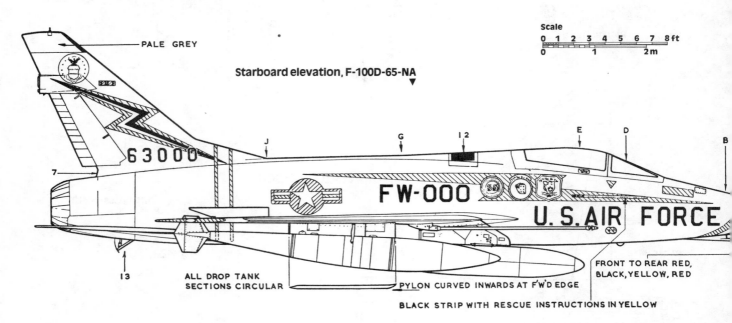

PALE GREY

Scale
0 1 2 3 4 5 6 7 8ft
0 1 2m

Starboard elevation, F-100D-65-NA ▼

63000

FW-000

U.S. AIR FORCE

ALL DROP TANK SECTIONS CIRCULAR

PYLON CURVED INWARDS AT F'W'D EDGE

FRONT TO REAR RED, BLACK, YELLOW, RED

BLACK STRIP WITH RESCUE INSTRUCTIONS IN YELLOW

Fuselage cross-sections ▼

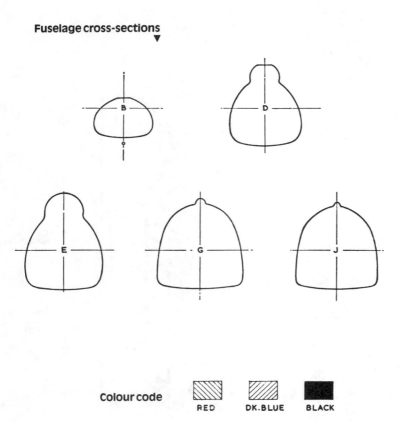

B

D

E

G

J

Colour code

RED   DK.BLUE   BLACK

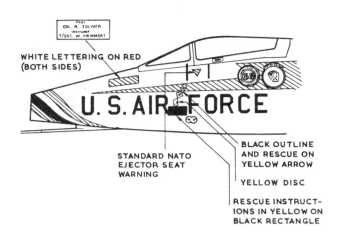

PILOT
COL. R. TOLIVER
CREW CHIEF
T/SGT. W. HEMMERT

WHITE LETTERING ON RED
(BOTH SIDES)

U.S. AIR FORCE

STANDARD NATO
EJECTOR SEAT
WARNING

BLACK OUTLINE
AND RESCUE ON
YELLOW ARROW

YELLOW DISC

RESCUE INSTRUCT-
IONS IN YELLOW ON
BLACK RECTANGLE

20 TH.T.F. WING
FIN BADGE.

Pale blue ground, white cloud and
base to black eagle. Shield dark
blue, yellow and red. Banner and
stars, yellow.

▲ ▶
Scrap views, F-100D-65-NA
*Details of markings applied to 56-3000A
as flown by Col R F Toliver, CO 20th TFW*

55 Squadron. All dark blue except for
white dice, numerals and border to yellow
title. 77 Squadron: Red ground, white
cards and name panel, black then white
circles on outside.

79 Squadron: White outline to pale
blue shield, white, black and orange
head, orange "sparks" with red
shading, red patch under orange claws

RED,WHITE,RED,
WARNING STRIPES

**The famous 'Triple Zilch', subject of George Cox's drawings –
surely the most colourful F-100 ever flown.**
▼

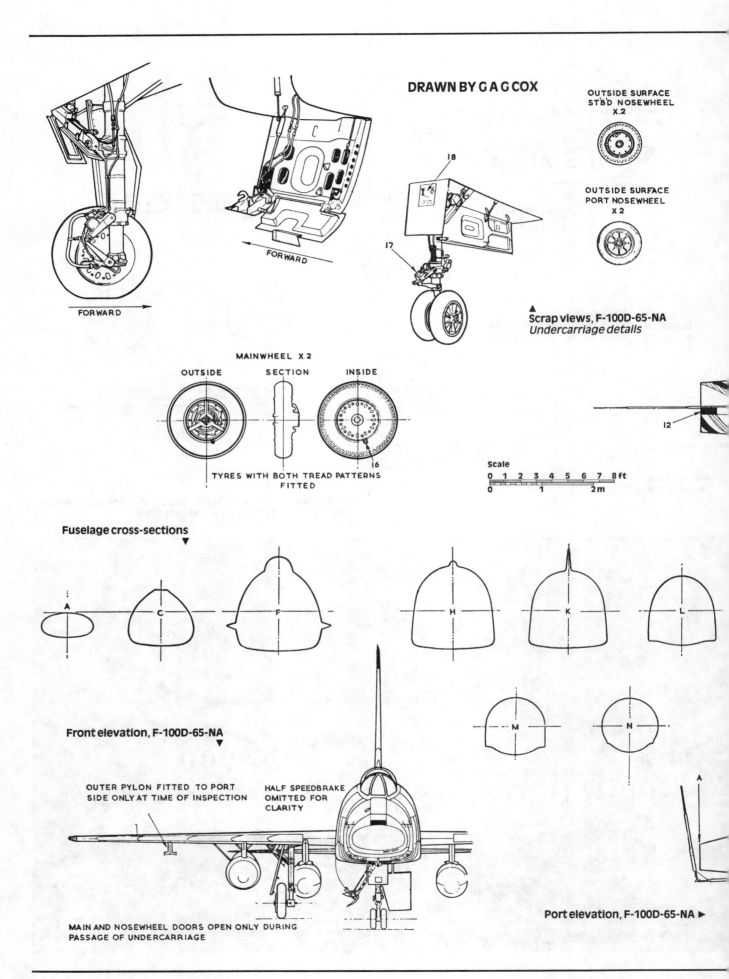

DRAWN BY G A G COX

OUTSIDE SURFACE
STB'D NOSEWHEEL
X.2

OUTSIDE SURFACE
PORT NOSEWHEEL
X 2

18

17

FORWARD

FORWARD

▲ Scrap views, F-100D-65-NA
Undercarriage details

12

MAINWHEEL X 2

OUTSIDE   SECTION   INSIDE

16

TYRES WITH BOTH TREAD PATTERNS
FITTED

Scale
0 1 2 3 4 5 6 7 8ft
0   1   2m

Fuselage cross-sections
▼

A   C   F   H   K   L

M   N

Front elevation, F-100D-65-NA
▼

OUTER PYLON FITTED TO PORT
SIDE ONLY AT TIME OF INSPECTION

HALF SPEEDBRAKE
OMITTED FOR
CLARITY

A

Port elevation, F-100D-65-NA ▶

MAIN AND NOSEWHEEL DOORS OPEN ONLY DURING
PASSAGE OF UNDERCARRIAGE

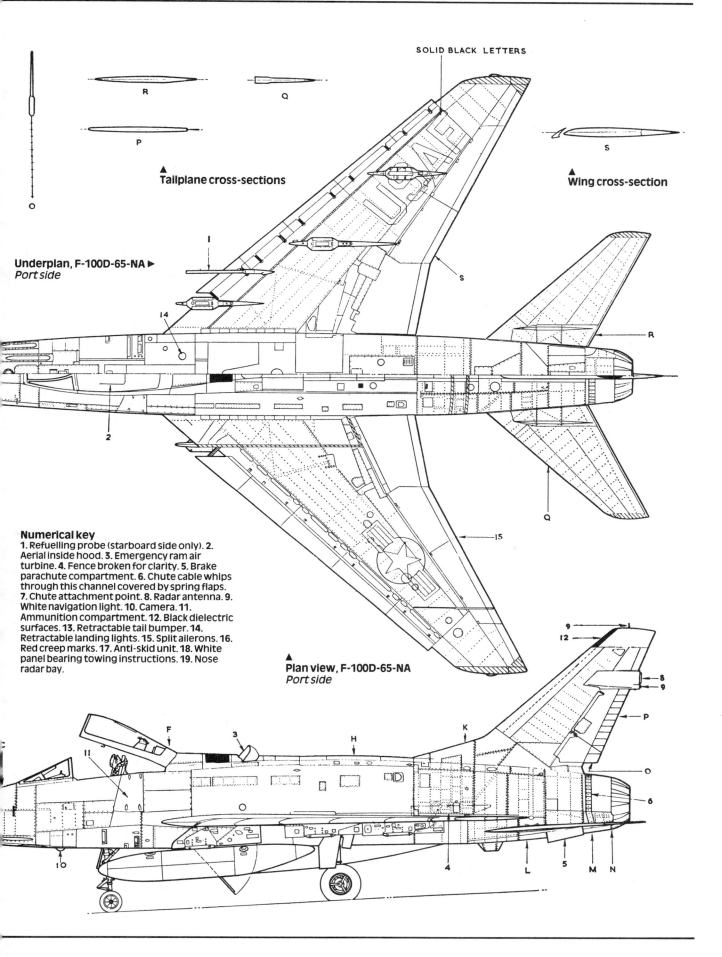

SOLID BLACK LETTERS

▲ Tailplane cross-sections

▲ Wing cross-section

R

Q

P

S

Underplan, F-100D-65-NA ►
Port side

14

2

15

R

S

Q

Numerical key
1. Refuelling probe (starboard side only). 2.
Aerial inside hood. 3. Emergency ram air
turbine. 4. Fence broken for clarity. 5. Brake
parachute compartment. 6. Chute cable whips
through this channel covered by spring flaps.
7. Chute attachment point. 8. Radar antenna. 9.
White navigation light. 10. Camera. 11.
Ammunition compartment. 12. Black dielectric
surfaces. 13. Retractable tail bumper. 14.
Retractable landing lights. 15. Split ailerons. 16.
Red creep marks. 17. Anti-skid unit. 18. White
panel bearing towing instructions. 19. Nose
radar bay.

▲ **Plan view, F-100D-65-NA**
Port side

9

12

8

9

P

O

6

F

3

H

K

11

10

4

L

5

M

N

Saab A32A Lansen

Country of origin: Sweden
Type: Two-seat, land-based all-weather attack fighter.
Dimensions: Wing span 42ft 8in *13.00m*; length 49ft 2in *14.99m*; height 16ft 5in *5.00m*.
Weights: Empty about 15,500lb *7030kg*; loaded about 22,000lb *10,000kg*.

Powerplant: One Svenska Flygmotor RM5 (Rolls-Royce Avon) axial-flow, afterburning turbojet of about 10,000lb *4535kg* maximum thrust.
Performance: Maximum speed over 700mph *1125kph*; initial climb rate about 12,000ft/min *3660m/min*; service ceiling 49,210ft *15,000m*; range (external fuel)

about 2000 miles *3200km*.
Armament: Four fixed Hispano Mk V 20mm cannon, plus up to 3000lb *1360kg* of external ordnance.
Service: First flight (prototype) 3 November 1952; service entry December 1955.

▲ The smooth lines of the Saab 32 are evident in this photo. A32A was the Lansen's Swedish Air Force designation.

DRAWN BY J ENOCH

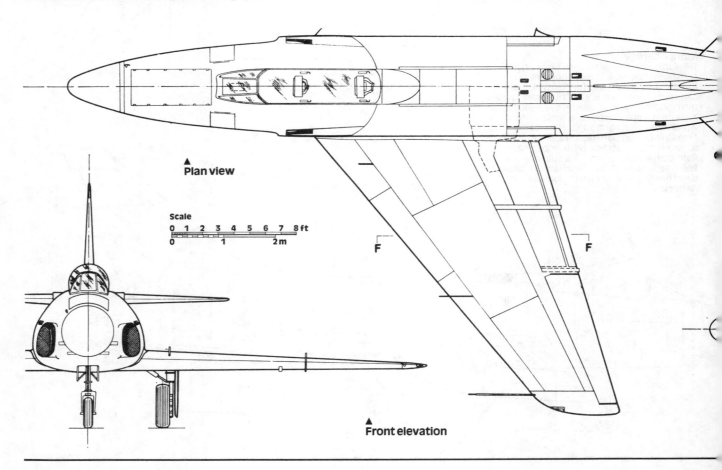

▲ Plan view

Scale

0 1 2 3 4 5 6 7 8 ft
0 1 2m

F   F

▲ Front elevation

▲
Early Lansens had a rounded tip to the fin leading edge,
modified on production aircraft to the square contours seen
here. 'Lansen' is Swedish for 'Lance'.

Wing and tailplane cross-sections
▼

A·A B·B   C·C D·D   E·E

F·F

G·G

▲
Fuselage cross-sections

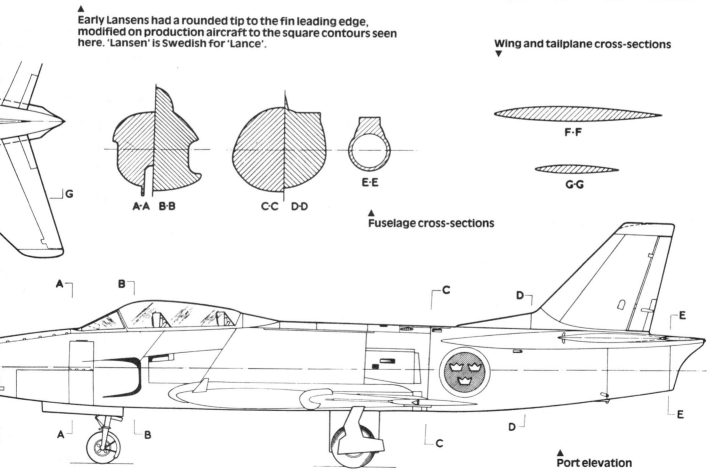

▲
Port elevation

21

Nord 1500 Griffon II

Country of origin: France.
Type: Experimental single-seat, land-based interceptor fighter.
Dimensions: Wing span 26ft 0in *7.93m*; length 46ft 0in *14.00m*; height 16ft 5in *5.00m*.

Weights: Loaded about 13,225lb *6000kg*.
Powerplant: One SNECMA Atar 101E axial-flow turbojet of 7715lb *3500kg* static thrust, plus one Nord ramjet.
Performance: Maximum speed 930mph *1500kph* at 10,825ft *3300m*; initial climb

rate 17,050ft/min *5200m/min*.
Armament: None.
Service: First flight (Griffon I) 20 September 1955, (Griffon II) 23 January 1957.

▲
Griffon II in flight, successor to the less powerful Griffon I. Ventral intakes are nowadays very fashionable, as on the F-16 and EFA, and canard foreplanes are also much in vogue.

Plan view, Griffon II
▼

Underplan, Griffon II
▼

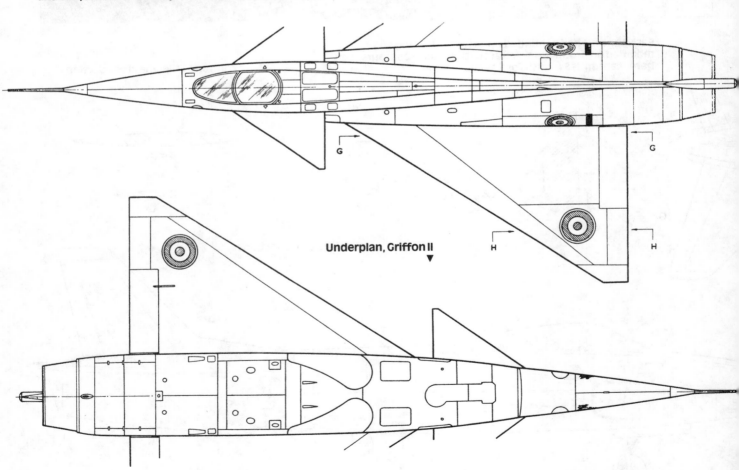

DRAWN BY E TAGE LARSEN

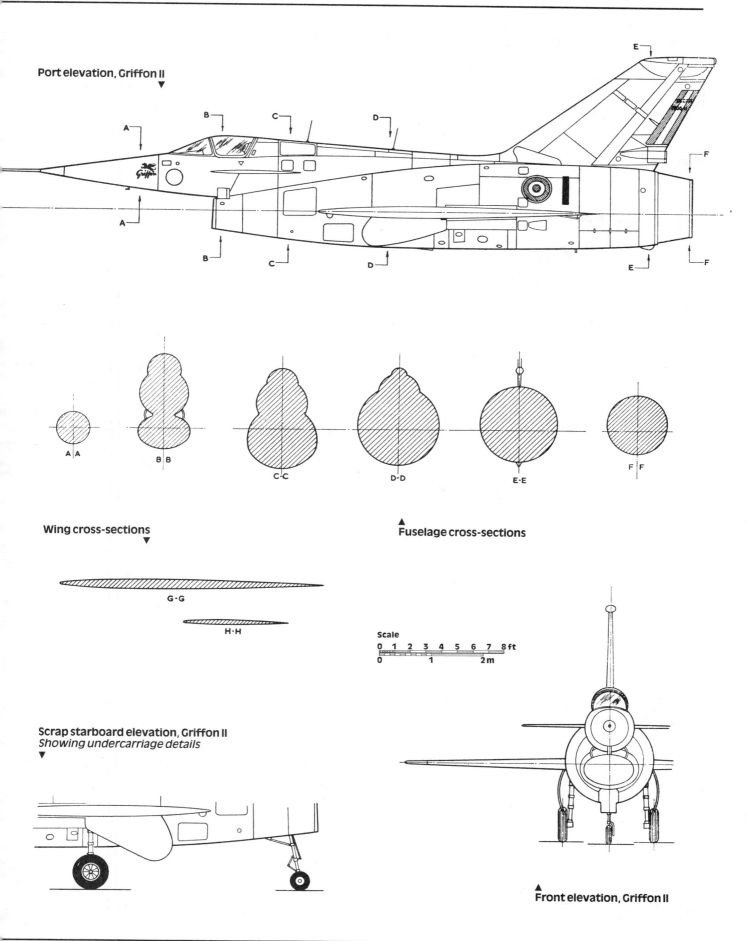

Port elevation, Griffon II

Wing cross-sections

Fuselage cross-sections

Scrap starboard elevation, Griffon II
Showing undercarriage details

Scale
0 1 2 3 4 5 6 7 8 ft
0   1   2 m

Front elevation, Griffon II

English Electric Canberra B(I) Mk 8

Country of origin: Great Britain.
Type: Long-range, land-based night interdictor or high-altitude bomber and target marker.
Dimensions: Wing span 63ft 11½in *19.49m*; length 65ft 6in *19.96m*; height 15ft 7in *4.75m* wing area 960 sq ft *89.17m²*.
Weights: Empty 23,165lb *10,510kg*;

normal 46,990lb *23,215kg*; maximum 50,990lb *23,135kg*.
Powerplant: Two Rolls-Royce Avon Mk 109 axial-flow turbojets each of 7500lb *3402kg* static thrust.
Performance: Maximum speed 560mph *902kph* at 40,000ft *12,190m*; initial climb rate 3600ft/min *1100m/min*; service ceiling 48,000ft *14,630m*; range about 800

miles *1300km*.
Armament: Four fixed 20mm Hispano cannon in detachable belly pack; up to 3000lb *1361kg* of bombs in fuselage bay, plus up to 2000lb *907kg* of bombs or rockets under wings.
Service: First flight (prototype) 13 May 1949, (Mk 8) 23 July 1954.

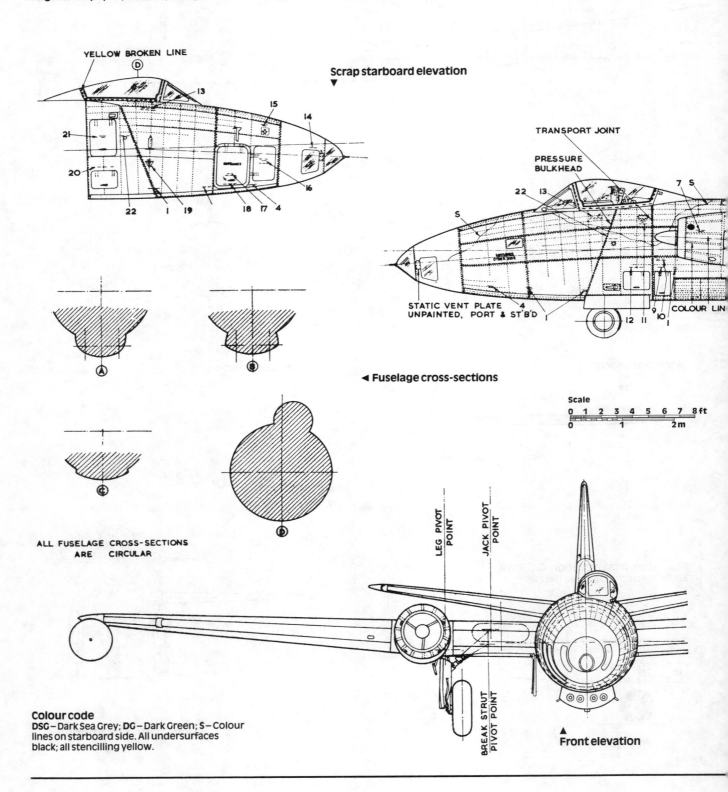

Scrap starboard elevation ▼

◀ Fuselage cross-sections

ALL FUSELAGE CROSS-SECTIONS ARE CIRCULAR

Scale

▲ Front elevation

Colour code
DSG – Dark Sea Grey; **DG** – Dark Green; **S** – Colour lines on starboard side. All undersurfaces black; all stencilling yellow.

B(I) Mk 8 XH234 at the 1957 Farnborough Air Show. Most of these interdictors were allocated to RAFG squadrons.

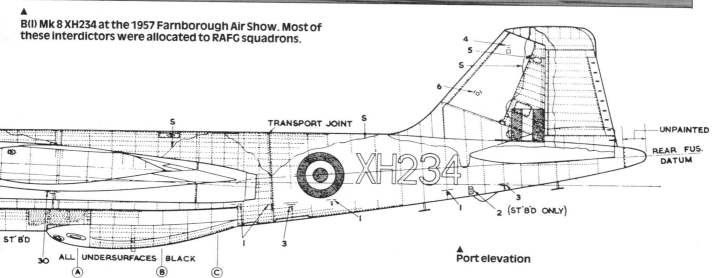

TRANSPORT JOINT

UNPAINTED

REAR FUS.
DATUM

2 (ST'B'D ONLY)

ST'B'D

ALL UNDERSURFACES BLACK

Ⓐ   Ⓑ   Ⓒ

▲
Port elevation

The B(I).8 prototype, VX185, was converted from the sole B Mk 5, the record-breaking 'double-crosser' of the Atlantic.
▼

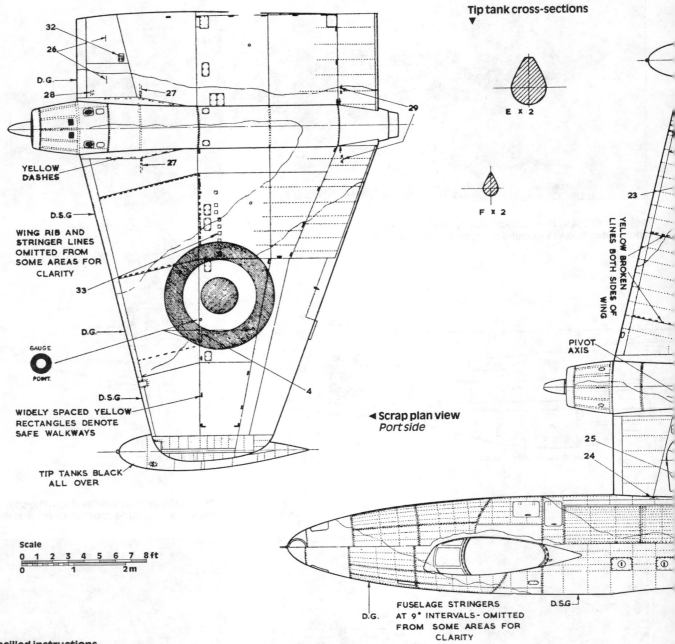

Tip tank cross-sections ▼

E x 2

F x 2

32
26
D.G.
28
27
27

YELLOW DASHES

D.S.G

WING RIB AND STRINGER LINES OMITTED FROM SOME AREAS FOR CLARITY

33

D.G.

GAUGE POINT.

D.S.G

WIDELY SPACED YELLOW RECTANGLES DENOTE SAFE WALKWAYS

TIP TANKS BLACK ALL OVER

4

29

Scale
0 1 2 3 4 5 6 7 8ft
0   1   2m

23

YELLOW BROKEN LINES BOTH SIDES OF WING

PIVOT AXIS

25
24

◄ *Scrap plan view*
Port side

FUSELAGE STRINGERS AT 9° INTERVALS - OMITTED FROM SOME AREAS FOR CLARITY

D.G.
D.S.G

FUS DATUM

LEG PIVOT POINT

NOSE SECTION DATUM

PORT WHEEL REMOVED

BREAK STR
PIVOT POIN

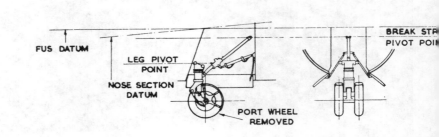

▲▶
Scrap views
Undercarriage details

Stencilled instructions
1. Trestle here. 2. Forward, Critical angle of attack normal to skin line 28°±1°. Do not damage. 3. Picketing lugs in here, Camera Hatch. 4. Sling here. 5. Æ conn. 6. Short Æ Long. 7. Debris guard lock. 8. Engine oil filler. 9. Oxygen charging valve inside. 10. Accumulators. 11. Hydraulic filler. 12. VHF TR units. 13. Chop thro canopy for emergency release. 14. Do not paint. 15. First aid inside (Red cross). 16. Wind break door. No entrance. 17. To open, press and turn. 18. Fire extinguisher inside. 19. Ejection seat warning (Red and white). 20. Ground supply socket 24 volts. 21. Equipment hatch. 22. Jacking point. 23. Picketing point. 24. Wing pick up. 25. Sling on wing pick up. 26. Equipment. 27. Sling on bridge 02/103 sht. 5 inside. 28. Gearbox oil fillers OM 71. 29. Sling under cross member. 30. Jacking point inside. 31. Fire panel (Red). 32. Cold air unit OM 71. 33. Finger air brakes.
Note: All lettering except that visible on drawings is 1in high; 'Entrance' and 'Entrance other side' are 2in high.

DRAWN BY G A G COX

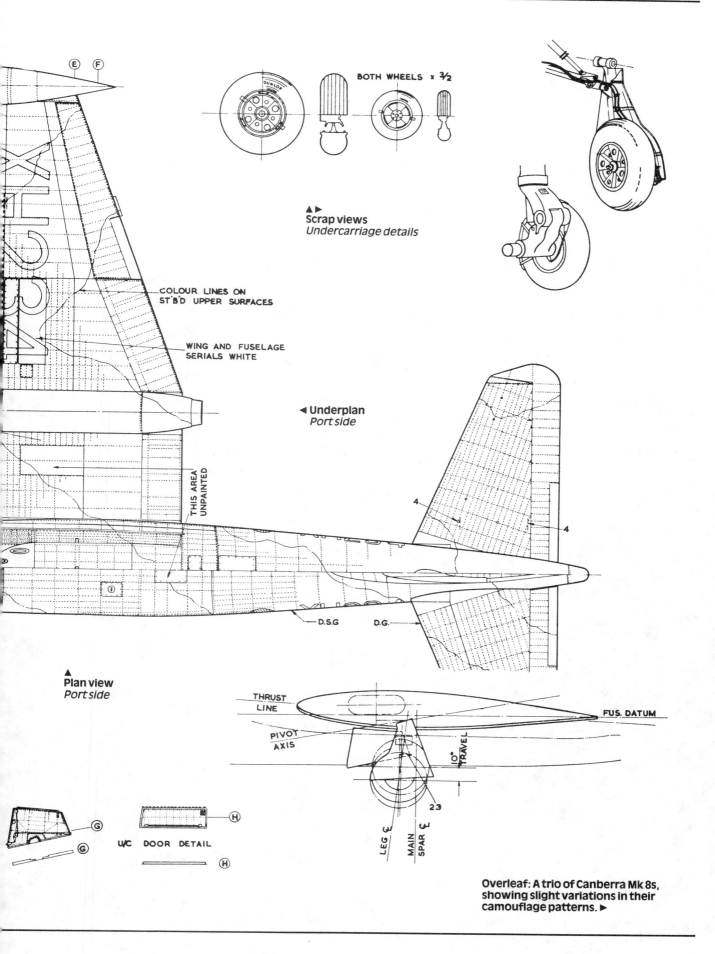

BOTH WHEELS x 3/2

▲ ► Scrap views
Undercarriage details

COLOUR LINES ON
ST'B'D UPPER SURFACES

WING AND FUSELAGE
SERIALS WHITE

◄ Underplan
Port side

THIS AREA
UNPAINTED

4

4

D.S.G   D.G.

▲ Plan view
Port side

THRUST
LINE

FUS. DATUM

PIVOT
AXIS

10° TRAVEL

23

LEG ℄   MAIN SPAR ℄

G

G

U/C DOOR DETAIL

H

H

**Overleaf: A trio of Canberra Mk 8s,
showing slight variations in their
camouflage patterns. ►**

Fiat G91

Country of origin: Italy.
Type: Single-seat, land-based light ground-attack fighter.
Dimensions: Wing span 28ft 1in *8.56m*; length 33ft 9½in *10.30m*; height 13ft 1½in *4.00m*; wing area 176.74 sq ft *16.42m²*.
Weights: Empty about 7200lb *3267kg*;

maximum take-off 12,125lb *5500kg*.
Powerplant: One Bristol Orpheus 801 turbojet of 4850lb *2200kg* static thrust.
Performance: Maximum speed 650mph *1045kph* at 4920ft *1500m*; initial climb rate about 6000ft/min *1800m/min*; service ceiling 40,000ft *12,190m*; range (clean, at sea level) about 400 miles

650km.
Armament: Four fixed 0.5in Colt-Browning machine guns, plus (optional) up to 1000lb *454kg* of external ordnance.
Service: First flight (prototype) August 1956; service entry February 1959.

Plan view
▼

Wing cross-sections
▼

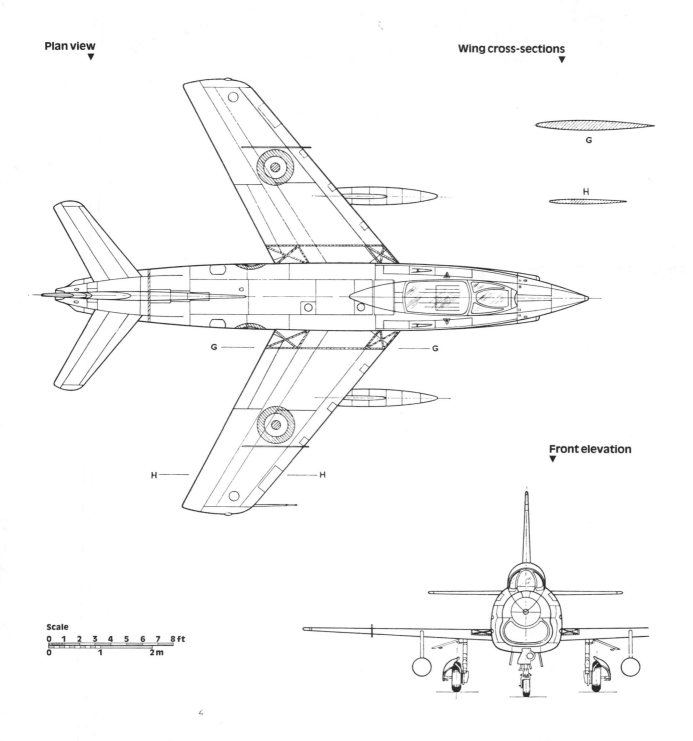

G

H

G   G

H   H

Front elevation
▼

Scale
0 1 2 3 4 5 6 7 8 ft
0   1   2 m

▲
Fiat (now Aeritalia) G91T two-seat trainer in Luftwaffe
service. The general similarity of the G91 design to that of the
F-86 Sabre was no accident.

Underplan
▼

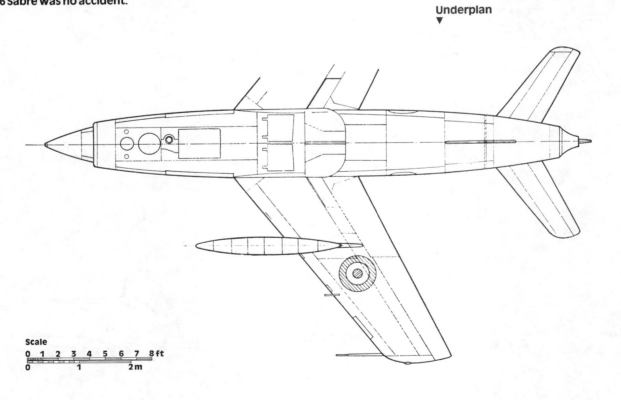

Scale
0 1 2 3 4 5 6 7 8 ft
0   1   2 m

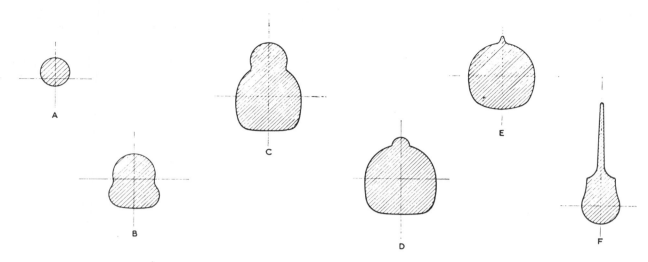

Fuselage cross-sections ▲

Port elevation ▲

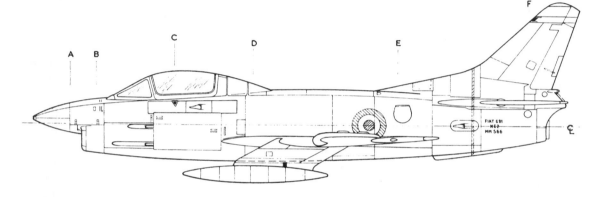

▲ **Scrap starboard elevation**
Showing undercarriage details

DRAWN BY E TAGE LARSEN

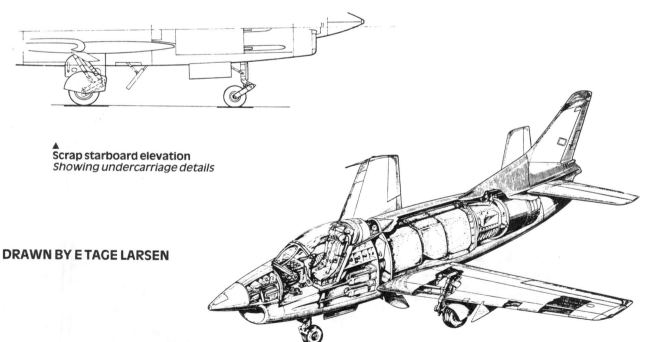

Fiat sectional drawing ▶

Lockheed CF-104 and F-104G Starfighter

Country of origin: USA.
Type: Single-seat, land-based strike fighter.
Dimensions: Wing span (without tip tanks) 21ft 11in *6.68m*; length 54ft 9in *16.69m*; height 13ft 6in *4.11m*; wing area 196.1 sq ft *18.22m²*.
Weights: Empty 14,082lb *6387kg*;

maximum take-off 28,779lb *13,054kg*.
Powerplant: One General Electric J79-GE-11A afterburning turbojet of 15,800lb *7170kg* maximum thrust.
Performance: Maximum speed 1450mph *2330kph* (Mach 2.2) at 36,000ft *10,975m*; initial climb rate 50,000ft/min *15,240m/min*; service ceiling 58,000ft *17,680m*;

range (ferry) 2180 miles *3500km*.
Armament: Two or four AIM-9 AAMs and (optional) one 20mm M61 cannon, or up to 4000lb *1820kg* of ordnance.
Service: First flight (XF-104) 28 February 1954, (F-104G) 5 October 1960, (CF-104) 26 May 1961.

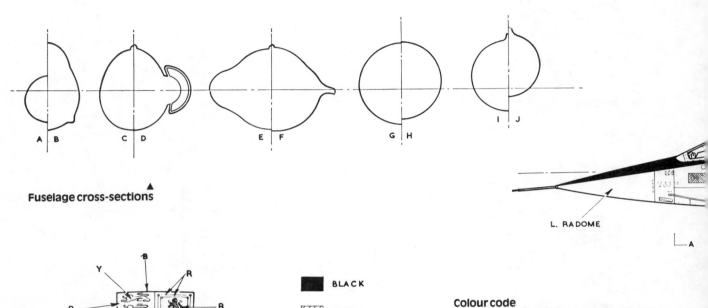

Fuselage cross-sections ▲

L. RADOME

I.
ON A R ENSIGN

BLACK

BLUE

RED

SMALL STENCILLING

Colour code
B – Black; **G** – Green; **L** – Light fawn; **R** – Red; **W** – White; **Y** – Yellow.
Note: Entire aircraft – polished metal; all radomes, anti-dazzle and dielectric panels matt.

CF-104 without wing-tip stores. Note slight drooping of movable wing surfaces.
▼

The first Dutch-built F-104G, prior to the application of national markings. White wing surfaces were typical of natural metal-finished Starfighters.

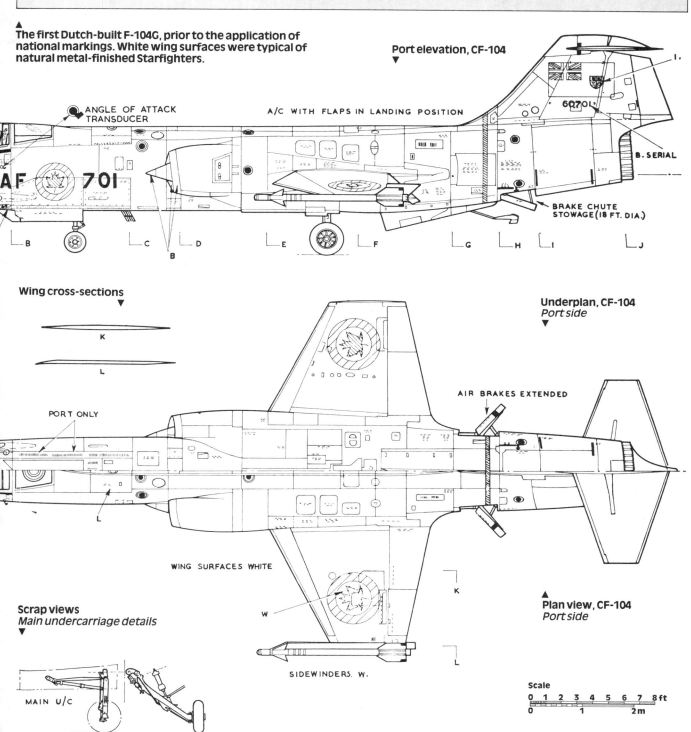

Port elevation, CF-104 ▼

ANGLE OF ATTACK TRANSDUCER

A/C WITH FLAPS IN LANDING POSITION

60-701

B. SERIAL

BRAKE CHUTE STOWAGE (18 FT. DIA.)

AF 701

B

B C D E F G H I J

Wing cross-sections ▼

K

L

Underplan, CF-104 *Port side* ▼

PORT ONLY

L

AIR BRAKES EXTENDED

WING SURFACES WHITE

W

K

L

SIDEWINDERS. W.

Plan view, CF-104 *Port side* ▲

Scrap views *Main undercarriage details* ▼

MAIN U/C

Scale

0 1 2 3 4 5 6 7 8 ft
0 1 2m

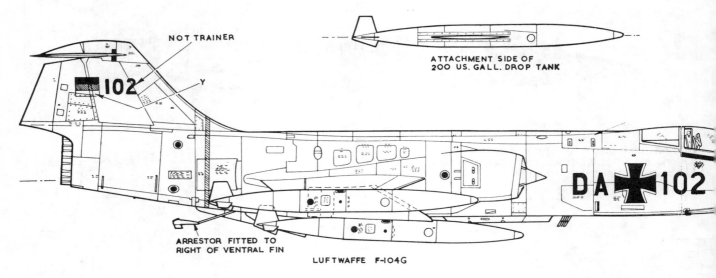

NOT TRAINER

ATTACHMENT SIDE OF
200 US. GALL. DROP TANK

Y

102

DA ✠ 102

ARRESTOR FITTED TO
RIGHT OF VENTRAL FIN

LUFTWAFFE F-104G

Starboard elevation, F-104G ▲

DRAWN BY D H COOKSEY

Scrap underplan, F-104G
▼

Front elevation, F-104G ▶

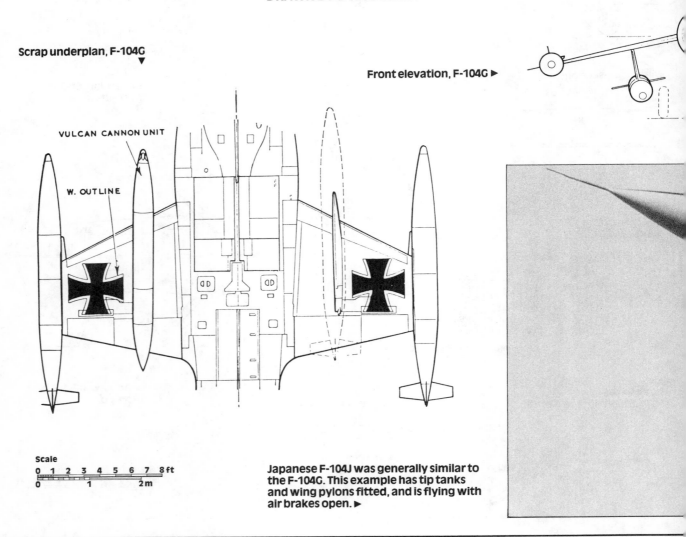

VULCAN CANNON UNIT

W. OUTLINE

Scale

0 1 2 3 4 5 6 7 8 ft
0   1   2 m

Japanese F-104J was generally similar to
the F-104G. This example has tip tanks
and wing pylons fitted, and is flying with
air brakes open. ▶

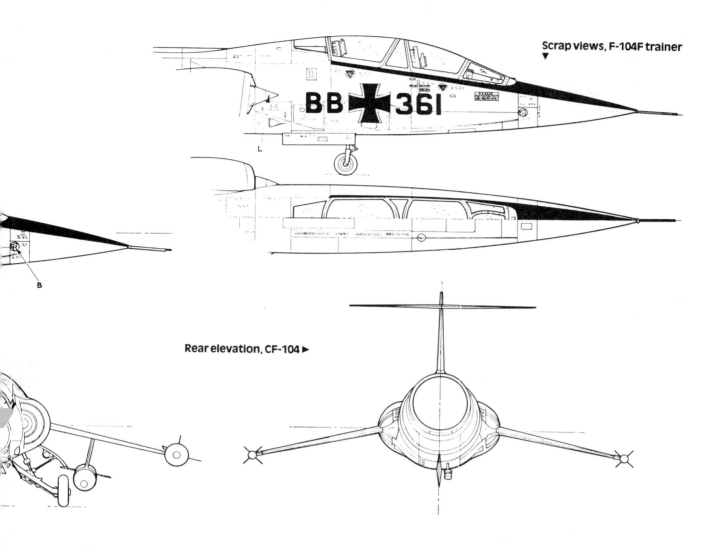

Scrap views, F-104F trainer ▼

BB ✠ 361

B

Rear elevation, CF-104 ▶

501

Saab J35A, SK35C and J35F Draken

Country of origin: Sweden.
Type: Single-seat, land-based fighter and (SK35C) trainer.
Dimensions: Wing span 30ft 10in *9.40m*; length 50ft 4in *15.35m*, (J35F) 52ft 0in *15.85m*; height 12ft 9in *3.9m*; wing area 529.6 sq ft *49.2m²*.
Weights: Empty (J35F) 18,185lb *8250kg*; loaded (J35A) 17,850–20,170lb *8100–9150kg*; maximum loaded (J35F) 27,050lb *12,275kg*.

Powerplant: One Svenska Flygmotor RM6 (Rolls-Royce Avon) afterburning turbojet of 15,000lb *6805kg* thrust, (J35F) RM6C of 17,635lb *8000kg* maximum thrust.
Performance: Maximum speed Mach 1.8 at altitude, (J35F) 1320mph *2125kph* (Mach 2.0) at altitude; initial climb rate about 39,370ft/min *12,000m/min*, (J35F) 49,210ft/min *15,000m/min*; service ceiling (J35F) 60,000ft *18,290m*; range

(clean) about 800 miles *1300km*, (maximum external fuel) about 2000 miles *3250km*.
Armament: (J35A, J35F) Two fixed 30mm Aden cannon, plus external ordnance up to 6830lb *3100kg*.
Service: First flight (prototype) 25 October 1955, (J35A) 15 February 1958, (SK35C) 30 December 1959; service entry (J35A) early 1960.

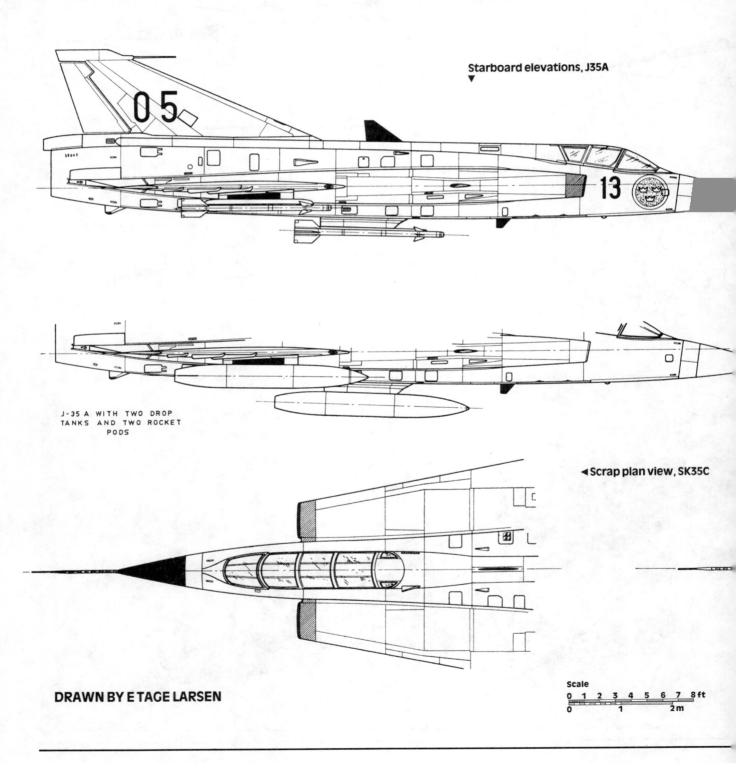

Starboard elevations, J35A ▼

J-35 A WITH TWO DROP TANKS AND TWO ROCKET PODS

◄ **Scrap plan view, SK35C**

DRAWN BY E TAGE LARSEN

Scale
0 1 2 3 4 5 6 7 8 ft
0 1 2 m

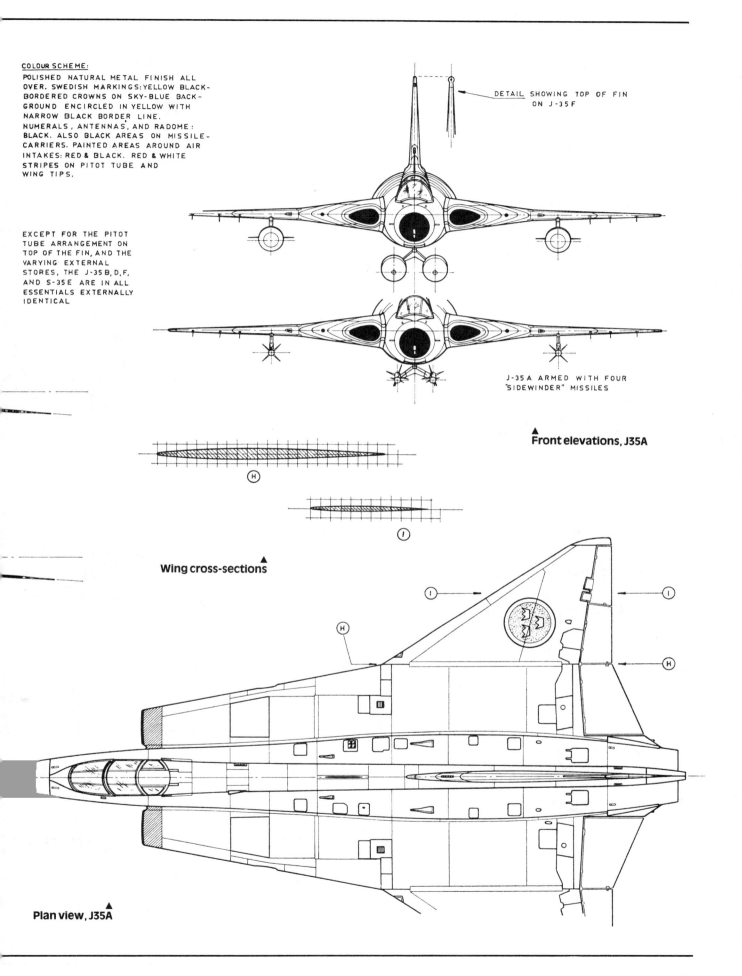

COLOUR SCHEME:
POLISHED NATURAL METAL FINISH ALL
OVER. SWEDISH MARKINGS: YELLOW BLACK-
BORDERED CROWNS ON SKY-BLUE BACK-
GROUND ENCIRCLED IN YELLOW WITH
NARROW BLACK BORDER LINE.
NUMERALS, ANTENNAS, AND RADOME:
BLACK. ALSO BLACK AREAS ON MISSILE-
CARRIERS. PAINTED AREAS AROUND AIR
INTAKES: RED & BLACK. RED & WHITE
STRIPES ON PITOT TUBE AND
WING TIPS.

EXCEPT FOR THE PITOT
TUBE ARRANGEMENT ON
TOP OF THE FIN, AND THE
VARYING EXTERNAL
STORES, THE J-35 B, D, F,
AND S-35 E ARE IN ALL
ESSENTIALS EXTERNALLY
IDENTICAL

DETAIL SHOWING TOP OF FIN
ON J-35F

J-35A ARMED WITH FOUR
"SIDEWINDER" MISSILES

▲ Front elevations, J35A

Wing cross-sections ▲

Plan view, J35A ▲

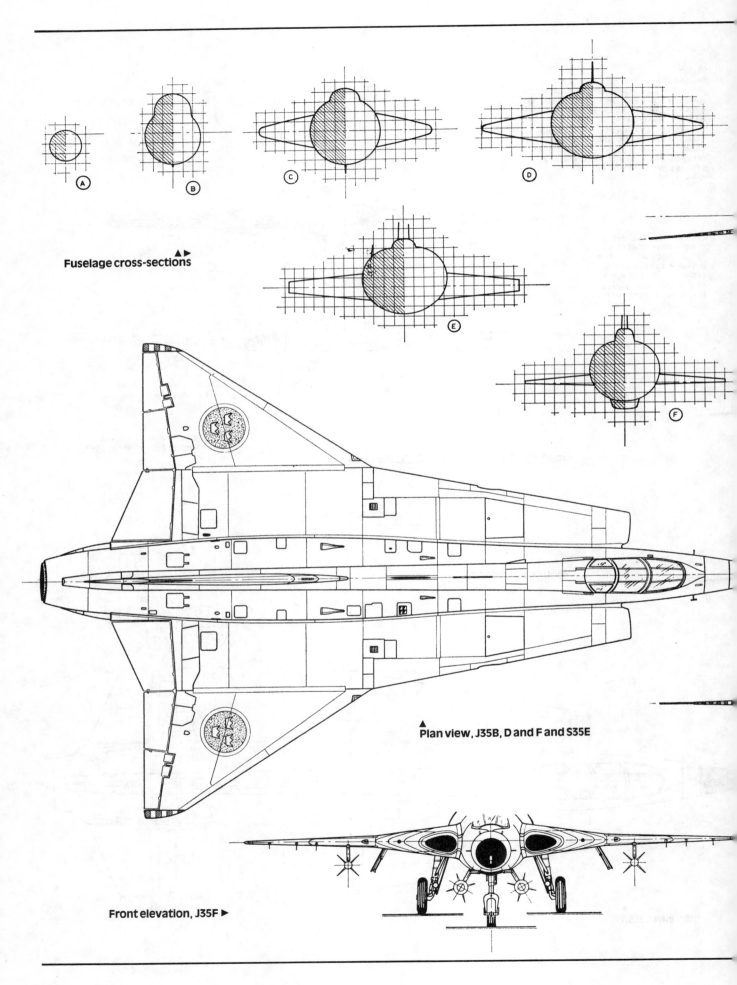

Fuselage cross-sections ▲▶

Plan view, J35B, D and F and S35E ▲

Front elevation, J35F ▶

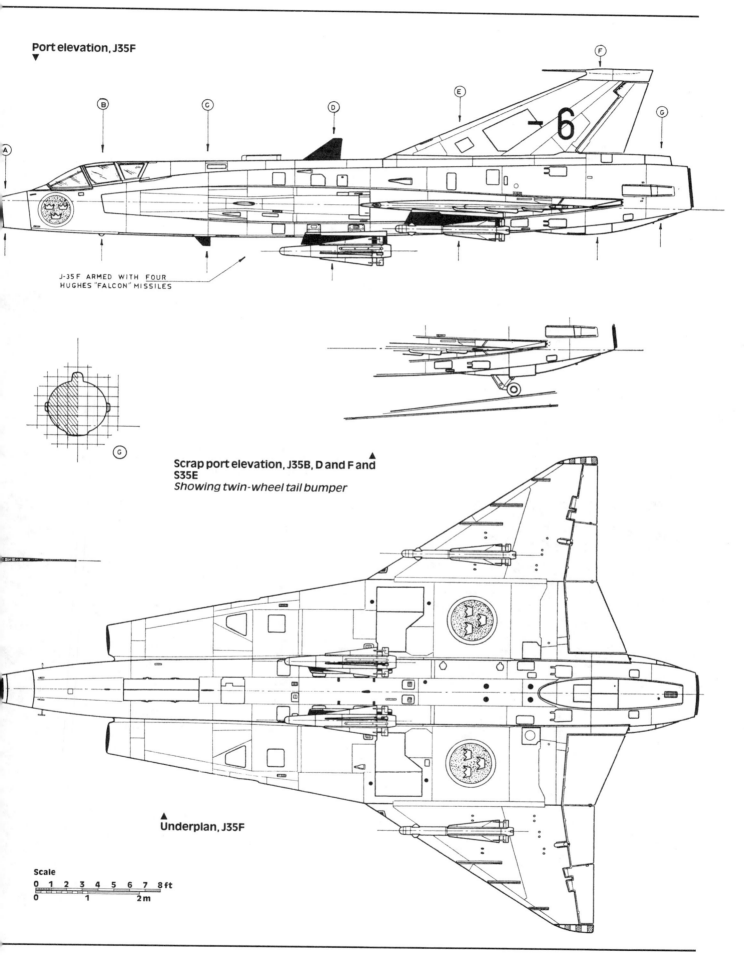

Port elevation, J35F
▼

–6

J-35F ARMED WITH <u>FOUR</u>
HUGHES "FALCON" MISSILES

G

▲ **Scrap port elevation, J35B, D and F and**
S35E
Showing twin-wheel tail bumper

▲ **Underplan, J35F**

Scale
0 1 2 3 4 5 6 7 8 ft
0   1   2 m

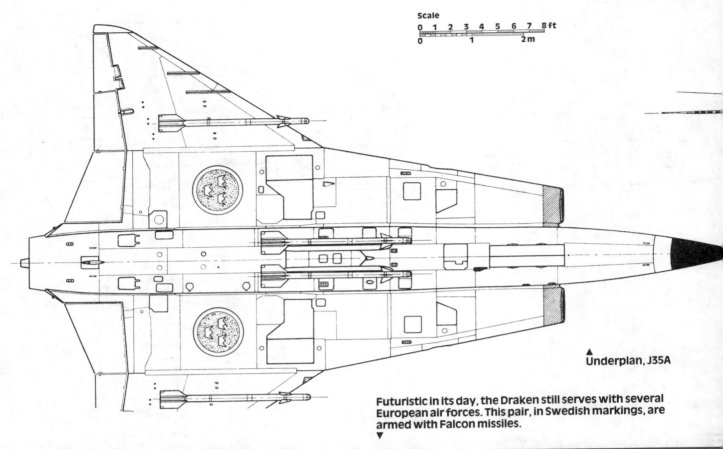

Scale

0 1 2 3 4 5 6 7 8 ft

0 1 2 m

▲ Underplan, J35A

Futuristic in its day, the Draken still serves with several European air forces. This pair, in Swedish markings, are armed with Falcon missiles.
▼

Port elevation, SK35C
▼

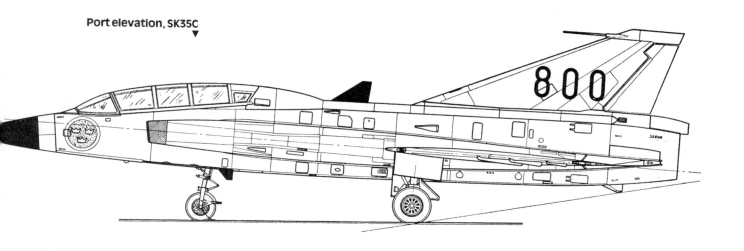

DETAIL SHOWING THE
NOSE WHEEL OF THE
-35 A,B,D,F, AND S-35E

ALTERNATE TYPE
OF WHEELS

◄ **Scrap views**
Undercarriage details

J-35A EQUIPPED WITH TWO FINNED 500 LITRE
(132 U.S. GAL.) DROP-TANKS, AND TWO PODS
EACH HOUSING 19 75 M.M. BOFORS ROCKETS

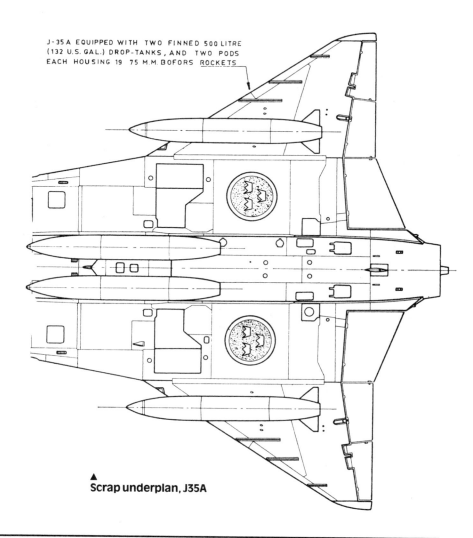

▲
Scrap underplan, J35A

Sukhoi Su-7B 'Fitter-A'

Country of origin: USSR
Type: Single-seat, land-based ground attack fighter.
Dimensions: Wing span 29ft 3½in *8.93m*; length (inc probe) 57ft 0in *17.37m*; height 15ft 0in *4.57m*.
Weights: Normal take-off 26,450lb *12,000kg*; maximum take-off 31,965lb

14,500kg.
Powerplant: One Lyulka AL-7F-1 afterburning turbojet of about 22,000lb *10,000kg* maximum thrust.
Performance: Maximum speed 1085mph *1750kph* (Mach 1.7) at 36,100ft *11,000m*; initial climb rate about 29,500ft/min *9000m/min*; service ceiling about

50,000ft *15,240m*; range about 900 miles *1450km*.
Armament: Two fixed 30mm cannon, plus up to about 2200lb *1000kg* of external ordnance.
Service: First flight (prototype) 1956; service entry about 1960.

DRAWN BY IAN R STAIR

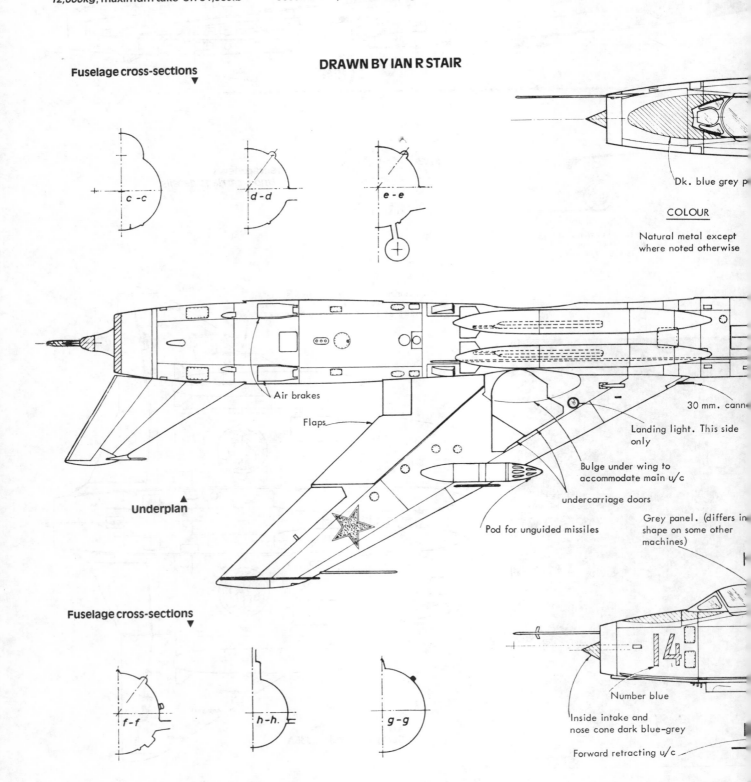

Fuselage cross-sections ▼

c - c

d - d

e - e

Dk. blue grey p

COLOUR

Natural metal except where noted otherwise

Air brakes

Flaps

Underplan ▲

30 mm. canne

Landing light. This side only

Bulge under wing to accommodate main u/c

undercarriage doors

Pod for unguided missiles

Grey panel. (differs in shape on some other machines)

Fuselage cross-sections ▼

f - f

h - h.

g - g

Number blue

Inside intake and nose cone dark blue-grey

Forward retracting u/c

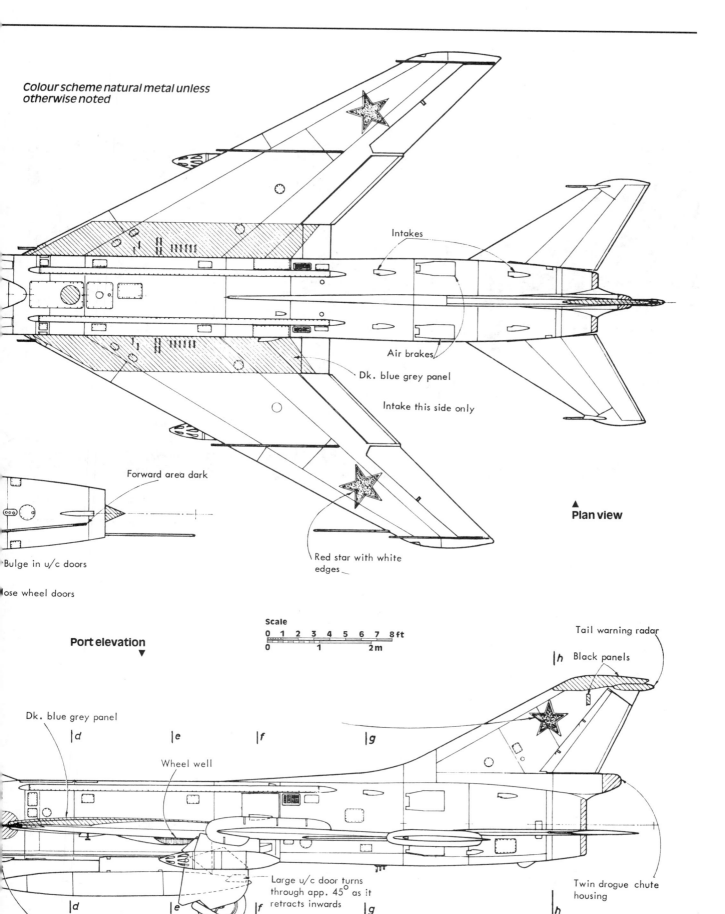

Colour scheme natural metal unless otherwise noted

Intakes

Air brakes

Dk. blue grey panel

Intake this side only

▲ **Plan view**

Forward area dark

Bulge in u/c doors

Nose wheel doors

Red star with white edges

Tail warning radar

|h   Black panels

Dk. blue grey panel

|d |e |f |g

Wheel well

Scale

0 1 2 3 4 5 6 7 8 ft

0   1   2 m

Port elevation ▼

Large u/c door turns through app. 45° as it retracts inwards

|d |e |f |g |h

Intake this side only

Twin drogue chute housing

Spectacular rocket-assisted take-off by an Su-7. A big, powerful fighter, the 'Fitter' had, by Western standards, only a modest armament.

Front elevation
▼

⌐a |b

⌐a |b Tyres black

Scale

0 1 2 3 4 5 6 7 8 ft

0   1   2 m

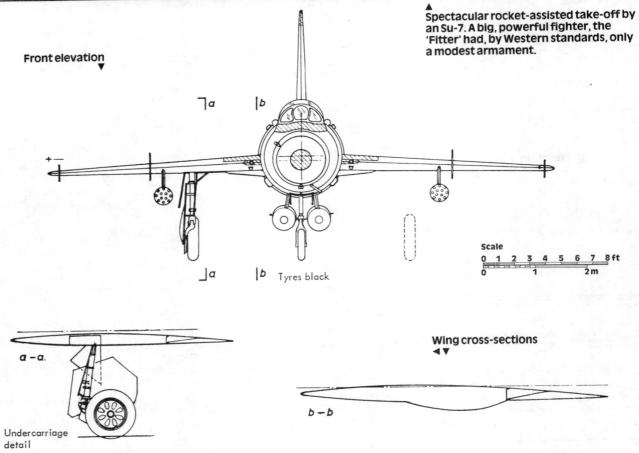

a – a.

Undercarriage detail

Wing cross-sections
◄▼

b – b

Macchi MB.326

Country of origin: Italy
Type: Two-seat, land-based trainer.
Dimensions: Wing span (over tip tanks) 34ft 8in *10.57m*; length 34ft 11¼in *10.65m*; height 12ft 2½in *3.72m*; wing area 204.52 sq ft *19.0m²*.
Weights: Empty 4930lb *2237kg*; maximum take-off 7347lb *3334kg*.

Powerplant: One Bristol Siddeley Viper 11 turbojet of 2500lb *1134kg* thrust.
Performance: Maximum speed 500mph *805kph* at 20,000ft *6100m*; initial climb rate 4500ft/min *1375m/min*; service ceiling 44,000ft *13,400m*; range 690 miles *1110km*.
Armament: (Optional) Two fixed 7.7mm

machine guns, plus up to 500lb *227kg* of bombs or rockets under wings.
Service: First flight (prototype) 10 December 1957, (production aircraft) 5 October 1960; service entry January 1962.

Port elevation, MB.326F
▼

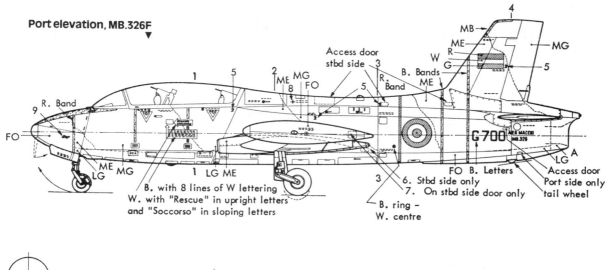

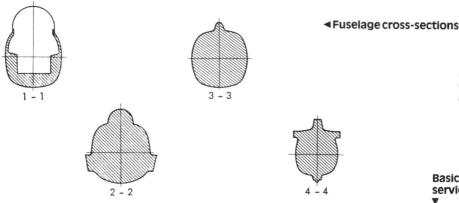

B. with 8 lines of W lettering
W. with "Rescue" in upright letters
and "Soccorso" in sloping letters

6. Stbd side only
7. On stbd side door only

◄ **Fuselage cross-sections**

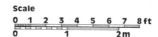

1 – 1

3 – 3

2 – 2

4 – 4

Scale
0 1 2 3 4 5 6 7 8 ft
0   1   2 m

Basic MB.326 trainer in Italian Air Force service. Colour scheme is orange overall.
▼

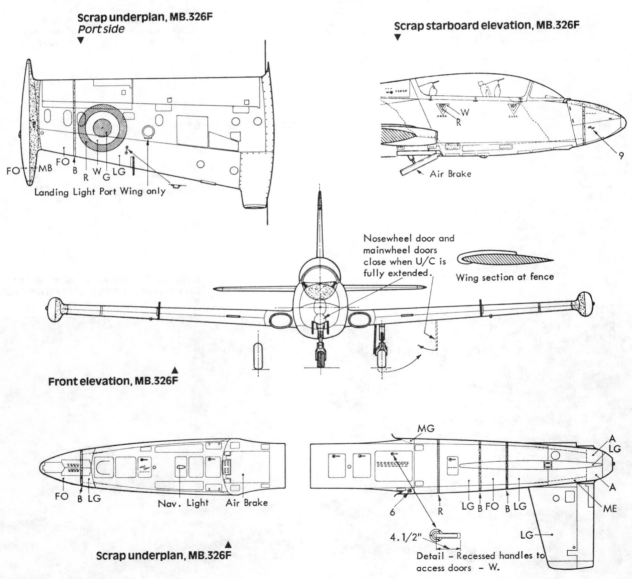

Scrap underplan, MB.326F
Port side ▼

FO MB FO B R W G LG

Landing Light Port Wing only

Scrap starboard elevation, MB.326F ▼

R W

Air Brake

9

Nosewheel door and
mainwheel doors
close when U/C is
fully extended.

Wing section at fence

Front elevation, MB.326F ▲

FO B LG

Nav. Light   Air Brake

Scrap underplan, MB.326F ▲

MG

A
LG

A

ME

6

R   LG B FO B LG

LG

4.1/2"

Detail - Recessed handles to
access doors - W.

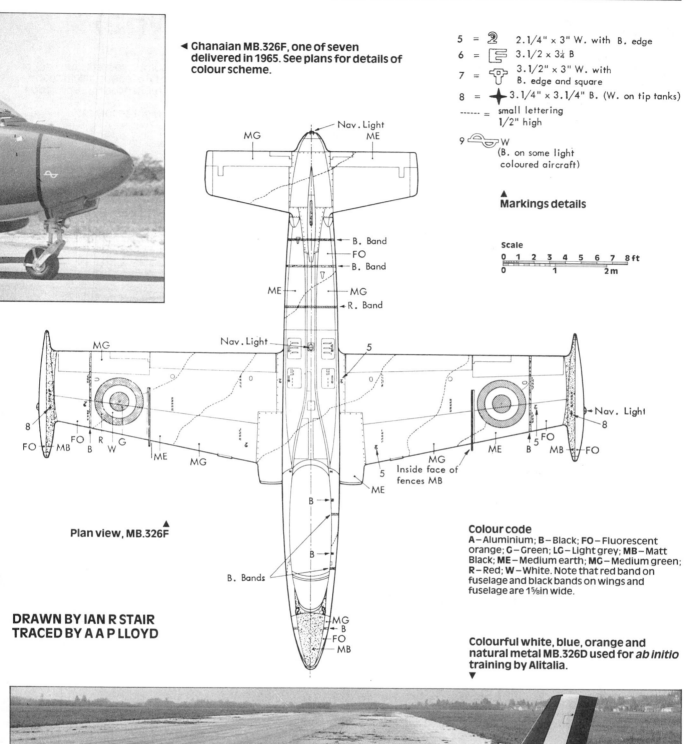

◄ Ghanaian MB.326F, one of seven delivered in 1965. See plans for details of colour scheme.

5 = 𝟚   2.1/4" × 3" W. with B. edge

6 = ⌐   3.1/2 × 3¼ B

7 = ⊤   3.1/2" × 3" W. with B. edge and square

8 = ✦   3.1/4" × 3.1/4" B. (W. on tip tanks)

------ = small lettering 1/2" high

9 ⬎W (B. on some light coloured aircraft)

▲ Markings details

Scale
0 1 2 3 4 5 6 7 8 ft
0   1   2 m

MG   Nav. Light   ME

B. Band
FO
B. Band

ME   MG
R. Band

MG   Nav. Light   5

8   Nav. Light   8

FO   FO   R   G   5 FO
MB   B   W   ME   ME   B   MB   FO
ME   MG   5   Inside face of fences MB   MG   ME

B

B

B. Bands

Plan view, MB.326F ▲

DRAWN BY IAN R STAIR
TRACED BY A A P LLOYD

MG
B
FO
MB

Colour code
A – Aluminium; B – Black; FO – Fluorescent orange; G – Green; LG – Light grey; MB – Matt Black; ME – Medium earth; MG – Medium green; R – Red; W – White. Note that red band on fuselage and black bands on wings and fuselage are 1⅝in wide.

Colourful white, blue, orange and natural metal MB.326D used for *ab initio* training by Alitalia.
▼

Northrop N-156F (F-5A prototype)

Country of origin: USA.
Type: Prototype single-seat, land-based light tactical fighter.
Dimensions: Wing span 25ft 3in *7.70m*; length 45ft 1in *13.74m*; height 13ft 1in *3.99m*; wing area 170 sq ft *15.79m²*.
Weights: Empty equipped about 8000lb *3630kg*; maximum about 20,000lb *9075kg*.

Powerplant: Two General Electric J85 afterburning turbojets each of 3850lb *1750kg* maximum thrust.
Performance: Maximum speed about 1000mph *1600kph* at 36,000ft *10,975m*; initial climb rate 28,700ft/min *8750m/min* at sea level; service ceiling 52,000ft *15,850m*; range (external fuel) about 1400

miles *2250km*.
Armament: Bombs, rockets, gun pack or AAMs up to total of about 2000lb *900kg* (considerably enhanced for production F-5A).
Service: First flight 30 July 1959.

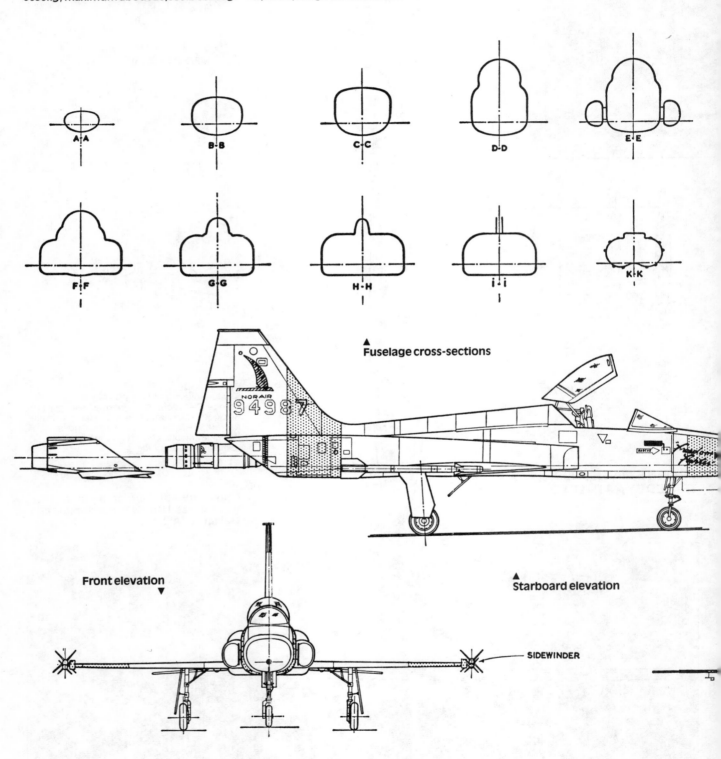

Fuselage cross-sections

Front elevation

Starboard elevation

SIDEWINDER

▲
N-156F, forerunner of a very successful lightweight fighter, the F-5. This view shows the aircraft equipped with wing-tip AIM-9s.

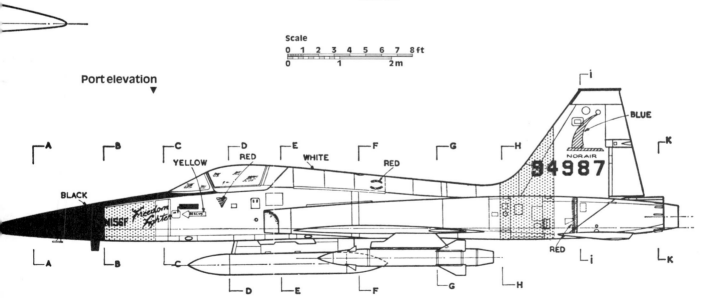

Scale

0 1 2 3 4 5 6 7 8 ft

0   1   2m

Port elevation
▼

BLUE

NORAIR

94987

A B C YELLOW D RED E WHITE F RED G H i K

BLACK

N156F   *Freedom Fighter*

RESCUE

RED

A B C D E F G H i K

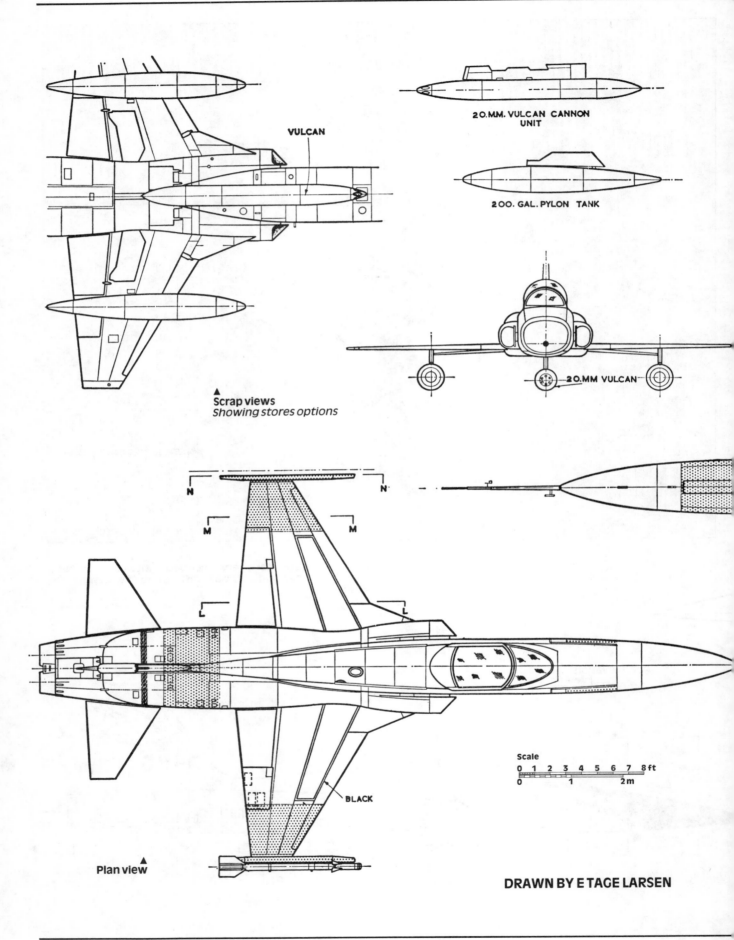

VULCAN

20.MM. VULCAN CANNON
UNIT

200. GAL. PYLON TANK

20.MM VULCAN

▲ Scrap views
Showing stores options

N   N

M   M

Scale
0 1 2 3 4 5 6 7 8 ft
0   1   2 m

BLACK

Plan view ▲

DRAWN BY E TAGE LARSEN

▲
The two-seat trainer variant of the N-156F became the T-38 Talon, which has seen widespread USAF service.

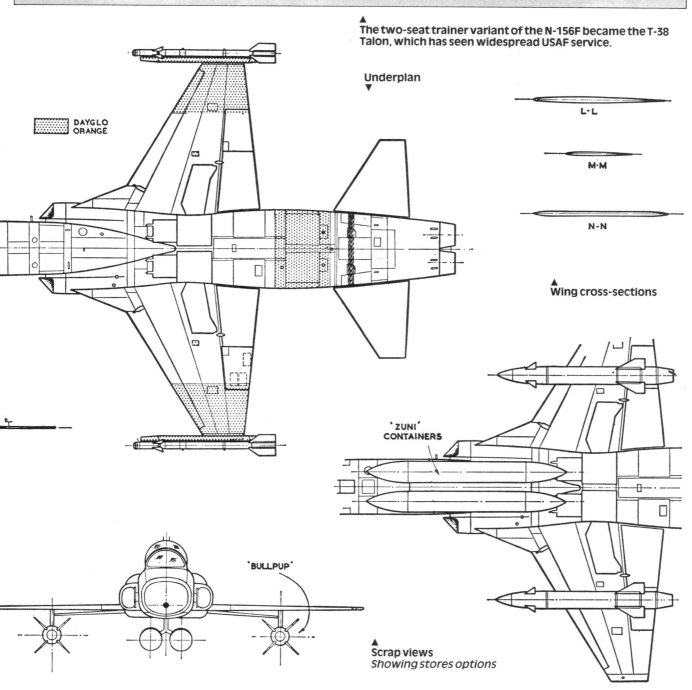

DAYGLO ORANGE

Underplan
▼

L-L

M-M

N-N

▲
Wing cross-sections

'ZUNI' CONTAINERS

'BULLPUP'

▲
Scrap views
Showing stores options

Handley Page Victor Mk 2

Country of origin: Great Britain.
Type: Long-range, land-based, strategic bomber, (SR Mk 2) strategic reconnaissance aircraft and (K Mk 2) tanker aircraft.
Dimensions: Wing span 120ft 0in *36.58m*; length 114ft 11in *35.03m*; height 30ft 1½in *9.18m*; wing area 2597 sq ft

241.22m².
Weights: (K Mk 2) Empty 110,310lb *50,050kg*; maximum 238,000lb *107,985kg*.
Powerplant: Four Rolls-Royce Conway RCo17 Mk 201 turbojets each of 20,600lb *9345kg* static thrust.
Performance: Maximum speed 610mph *982kph*; service ceiling 55,000ft *16,765m*;

range (at altitude) 4600 miles *7400km*.
Armament: Thirty-five 1000lb *454kg* bombs or one HS Blue Steel stand-off nuclear missile or other ordnance up to about 30,000lb *13,600kg*, (SR, K Mk 2) none.
Service: First flight 20 February 1959; service entry February 1962.

◄ **Victor B.2 in low-level camouflage. The tip of the Blue Steel missile can just be made out.**

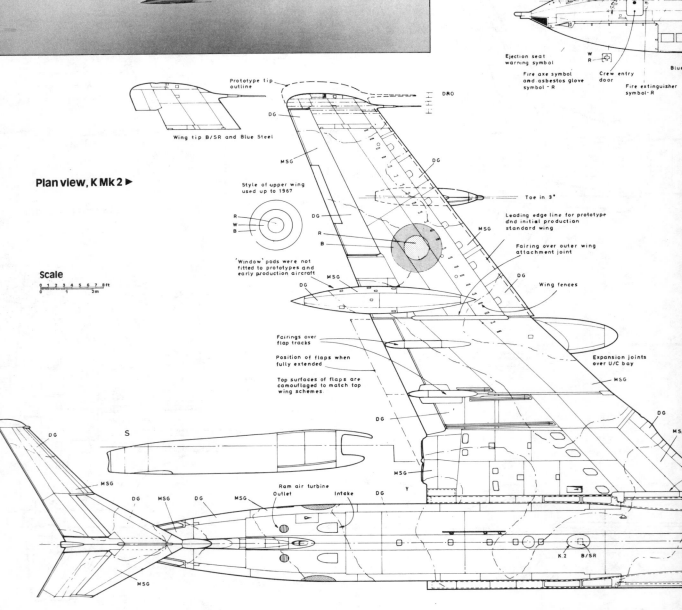

52

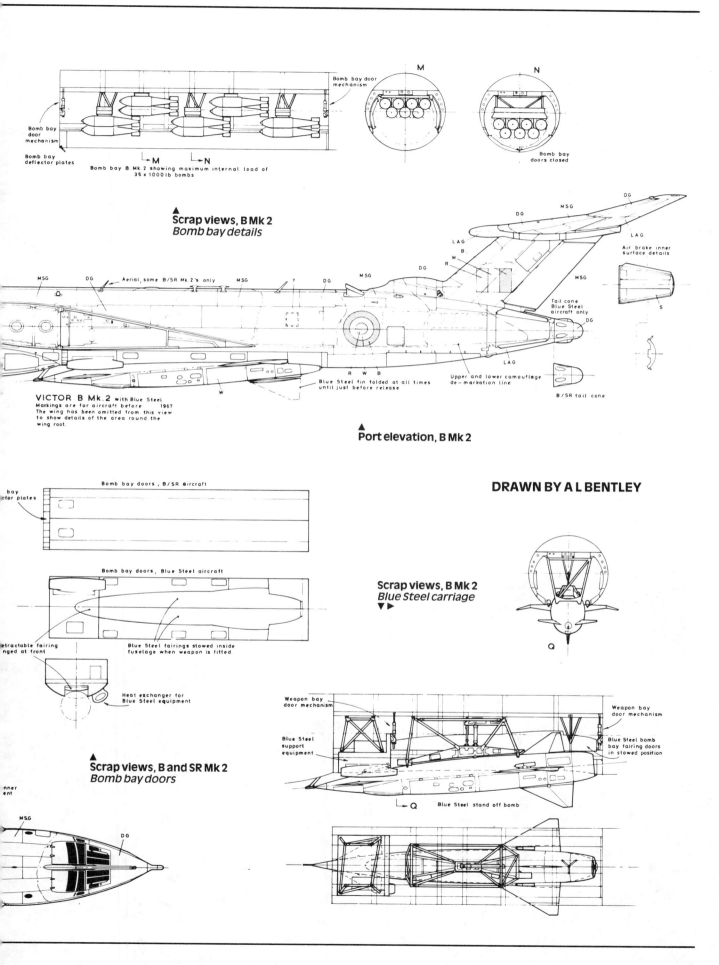

Bomb bay door mechanism

Bomb bay door mechanism

Bomb bay door mechanism

M

N

Bomb bay deflector plates

Bomb bay doors closed

Bomb bay B Mk 2 showing maximum internal load of 35 x 1000 lb bombs

▲ Scrap views, B Mk 2
Bomb bay details

MSG

DG

Aerial, some B/SR Mk 2's only

MSG

Y

DG

MSG

DG

LAG

B

R

W

MSG

DG

DG

MSG

DG

LAG

Air brake inner surface details

Tail cone Blue Steel aircraft only

S

R W B

Blue Steel fin folded at all times until just before release

Upper and lower camouflage de-markation line

LAG

B/SR tail cone

VICTOR B Mk.2 with Blue Steel
Markings are for aircraft before 1967
The wing has been omitted from this view to show details of the area round the wing root.

▲ Port elevation, B Mk 2

Bomb bay doors, B/SR aircraft

bay
ctor plates

DRAWN BY A L BENTLEY

Bomb bay doors, Blue Steel aircraft

etractable fairing
nged at front

Blue Steel fairings stowed inside fuselage when weapon is fitted

Heat exchanger for Blue Steel equipment

Scrap views, B Mk 2
Blue Steel carriage
▼ ►

Q

▲ Scrap views, B and SR Mk 2
Bomb bay doors

nner
ent

MSG

DG

Weapon bay door mechanism

Weapon bay door mechanism

Blue Steel support equipment

Blue Steel bomb bay fairing doors in stowed position

Q

Blue Steel stand off bomb

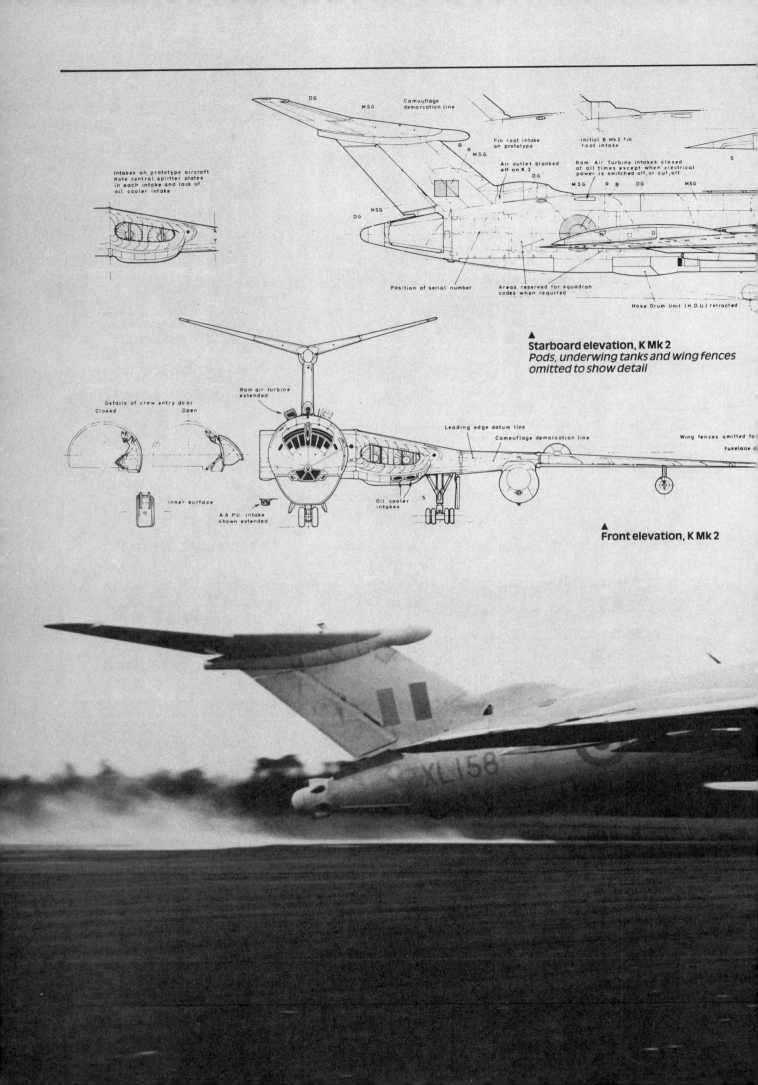

Intakes on prototype aircraft
Note central splitter plates
in each intake and lack of
oil cooler intake

DG
MSG
Camouflage
demarcation line

Fin root intake
on prototype

Initial B.Mk 2 fin
root intake

B
R
M.S.G.

Air outlet blanked
off on K.2

Ram Air Turbine intakes closed
at all times except when electrical
power is switched off,or cut,off

DG

S

MSG   R B   DG   MSG

DG

MSG

Position of serial number

Areas reserved for squadron
codes when required

Hose Drum Unit (H.D.U.) retracted

▲ **Starboard elevation, K Mk 2**
*Pods, underwing tanks and wing fences
omitted to show detail*

Details of crew entry door
Closed   Open

Ram air turbine
extended

Leading edge datum line

Camouflage demarcation line

Wing fences omitted for

Fuselage

inner surface

A A P U intake
shown extended

Oil cooler
intakes

S

▲ **Front elevation, K Mk 2**

XL158

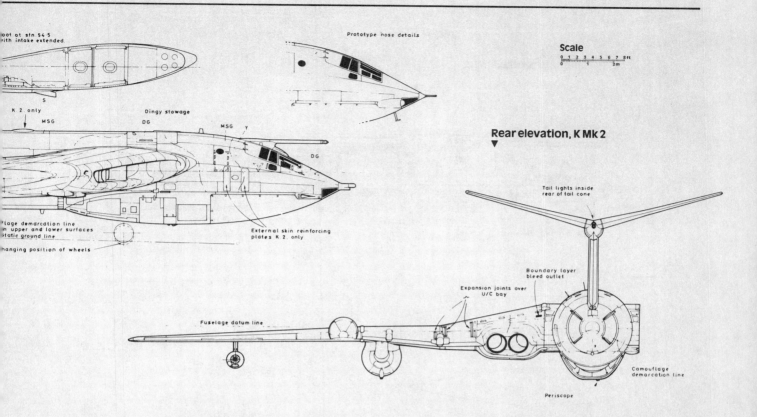

root at stn 54·5
with intake extended.

S

K 2 only

MSG

Dingy stowage
DG

Prototype hose details

MSG Y

DG

flage demarcation line
n upper and lower surfaces
static ground line

hanging position of wheels

External skin reinforcing
plates K 2. only

Scale

0 1 2 3 4 5 6 7 8 9 ft
0   1   2m

Rear elevation, K Mk 2
▼

Tail lights inside
rear of tail cone

Boundary layer
bleed outlet

Expansion joints over
U/C bay

Fuselage datum line

Periscope

Camouflage
demarcation line

**The first operational Victors were finished in anti-flash white,
with pink, white and pale blue national markings.**
▼

Port inboard profile, K Mk 2
▼

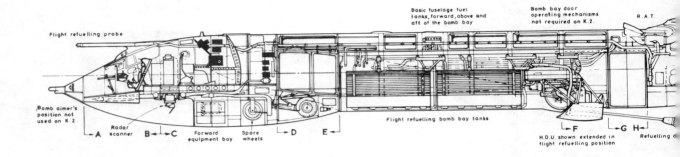

Flight refuelling probe

Basic fuselage fuel tanks, forward, above and aft of the bomb bay

Bomb bay door operating mechanisms not required on K.2.

R.A.T.

Bomb aimer's position not used on K.2

Radar scanner

Forward equipment bay

Spare wheels

Flight refuelling bomb bay tanks

H.D.U. shown extended in flight refuelling position

Refuelling

A — B — C   D   E   F — G H

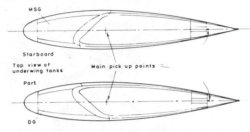

MSG

Starboard

Top view of underwing tanks

Port

DG

Main pick up points

Tank is same for both wings, only tank to wing fairing is handed. Tanks fitted to all Mk.2 aircraft except prototypes

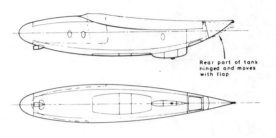

Rear part of tank hinged and moves with flap

▲
Scrap views
Underwing tanks

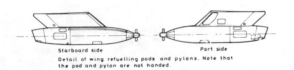

Starboard side   Port side

Detail of wing refuelling pods and pylons. Note that the pod and pylon are not handed.

Inboard view of wing-mounted refuelling pod, Victor K Mk 2, showing prominent dayglo stripes.
▼

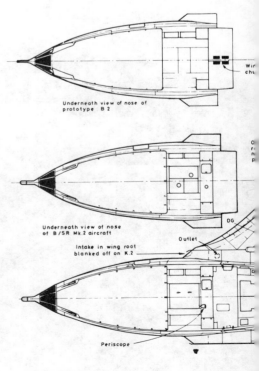

Wir chu

Underneath view of nose of prototype B 2

Or n p

Underneath view of nose of B/SR Mk.2 aircraft

DG

Intake in wing root blanked off on K.2

Outlet

Periscope

▼

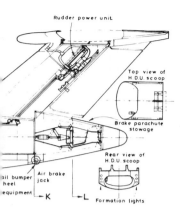

Rudder power unit
Top view of H.D.U. scoop
Brake parachute stowage
Rear view of H.D.U. scoop
Tail bumper
Air brake jack
Wheel equipment
K
L
Formation lights

Colour code
R – Red; **W** – White; **B** – Blue; **DG** – Dark Green; **MSG** – Medium Sea Grey; **LAG** – Light Aircraft Grey; **B** – Black; **S** – Silver; **DRO** – Dayglo red-orange; **Y** – Yellow; **NM** – Natural metal. Walkway areas at wing roots and on tailplane are outlined with a continuous, ¼in thick yellow line with a fringe of red stripes.

Scale
0 1 2 3 4 5 6 7 8ft
0 1 2m

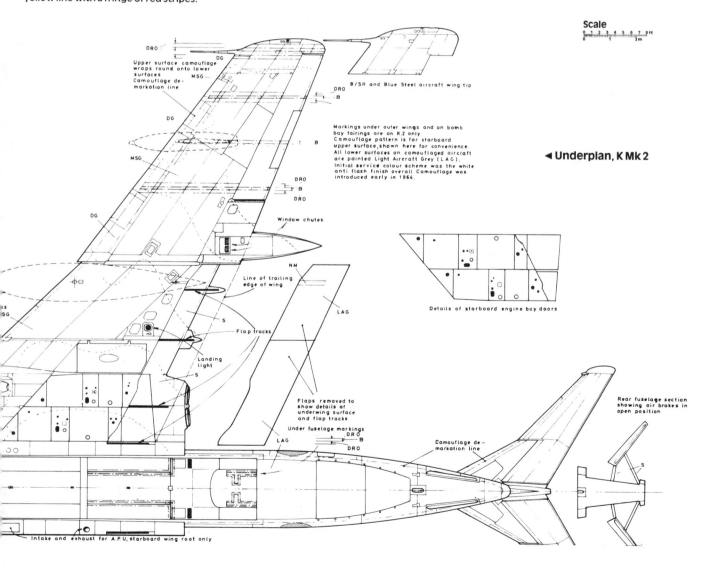

DRO
DG
Upper surface camouflage wraps round onto lower surfaces
Camouflage de-markation line
MSG
DG
MSG
DG

B/SR and Blue Steel aircraft wing tip

DRO
B

Markings under outer wings and on bomb bay fairings are on K.2 only
Camouflage pattern is for starboard upper surface, shown here for convenience. All lower surfaces on camouflaged aircraft are painted Light Aircraft Grey (LAG). Initial service colour scheme was the white anti flash finish overall Camouflage was introduced early in 1964.

◀ **Underplan, K Mk 2**

DRO
B
DRO

Window chutes

NM

Line of trailing edge of wing

LAG

S

Flap tracks

Landing light

S

Details of starboard engine bay doors

Flaps removed to show details of underwing surface and flap tracks

Under fuselage markings
DRO
B
DRO

LAG

Camouflage de-markation line

Rear fuselage section showing air brakes in open position

S

Intake and exhaust for A.P.U., starboard wing root only

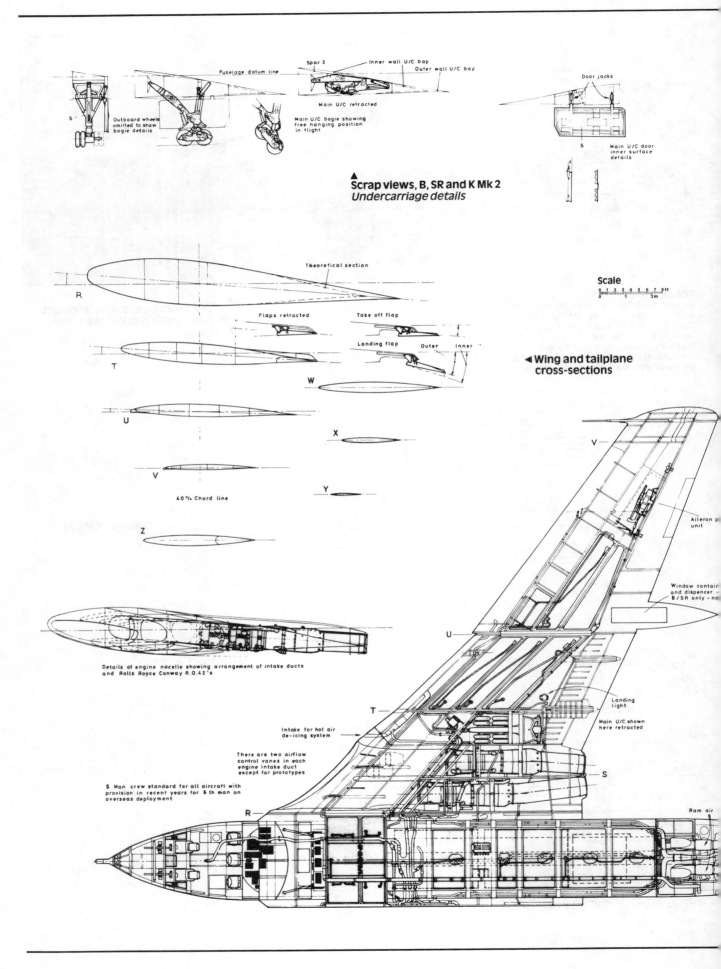

Spar 3

Inner wall U/C bay

Outer wall U/C bay

Fuselage datum line

Main U/C retracted

S

Outboard wheels omitted to show bogie details

Main U/C bogie showing free hanging position in flight

Door jacks

S

Main U/C door inner surface details

▲ **Scrap views, B, SR and K Mk 2**
Undercarriage details

Theoretical section

R

Scale

0 1 2 3 4 5 6 7 8ft
0   1   2m

Flaps retracted

Take off flap

T

Landing flap

Outer   Inner

W

◄ **Wing and tailplane cross-sections**

U

40% Chord line

X

V

Y

Z

V

Aileron p
unit

Window contain
and dispencer -
B/SR only - no

U

Details of engine nacelle showing arrangement of intake ducts and Rolls Royce Conway R.O.42's

Landing light

Main U/C shown here retracted

T

Intake for hot air de-icing system

S

There are two airflow control vanes in each engine intake duct except for prototypes

5 Man crew standard for all aircraft with provision in recent years for 6 th man on overseas deployment

R

Ram air

▲
Victor SR.2s at Wyton. As nuclear/
conventional strategic bombers, then
reconnaissance platforms and now
aerial tankers, Victors have certainly
given value for money.

◄ Inboard plan view, K Mk 2

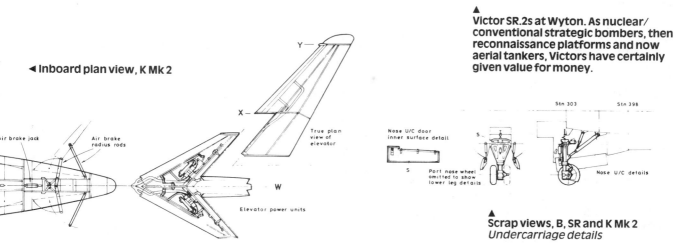

Air brake jack

Air brake
radius rods

Y —

X —

True plan
view of
elevator

W

Elevator power units

Nose U/C door
inner surface detail

Port nose wheel
omitted to show
lower leg details

Stn 303   Stn 398

Nose U/C details

▲
Scrap views, B, SR and K Mk 2
Undercarriage details

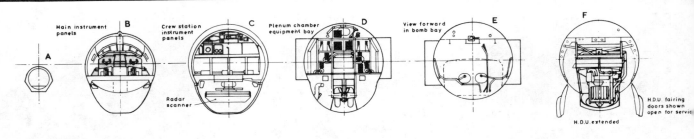

Main instrument panels — B

Crew station instrument panels — C

Plenum chamber equipment bay — D

View forward in bomb bay — E

F

A

Radar scanner

H.D.U. extended

H.D.U. fairing doors shown open for servic

Scale 0 1 2 3 4 5 6 7 8 ft
0 1 2 m

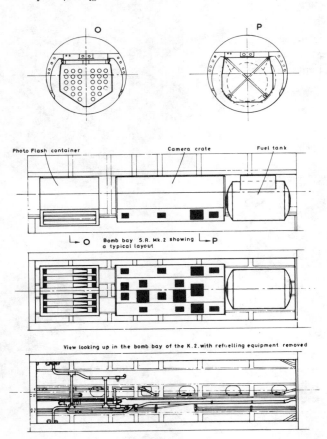

O

P

Photo Flash container

Camera crate

Fuel tank

→ O Bomb bay S.R. Mk.2 showing ← P
a typical layout

View looking up in the bomb bay of the K.2. with refuelling equipment removed

▲ **Scrap views, SR and K Mk 2**
Bomb bay details

Co-pilot's position, Victor K.2. Only the pilot and co-pilot have ejection seats.
▼

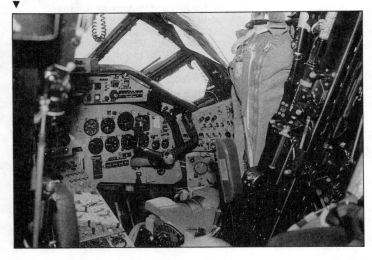

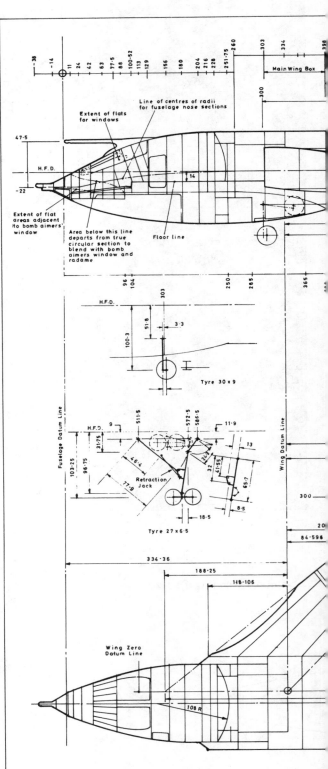

Main Wing Box

Line of centres of radii
for fuselage nose sections

Extent of flats
for windows

H.F.D.

Extent of flat
areas adjacent
to bomb aimers'
window

Area below this line
departs from true
circular section to
blend with bomb
aimers window and
radome

Floor line

H.F.D.

Tyre 30 x 9

Fuselage Datum Line

Wing Datum Line

H.F.D.

Retraction
Jack

Tyre 27 x 6.5

Wing Zero
Datum Line

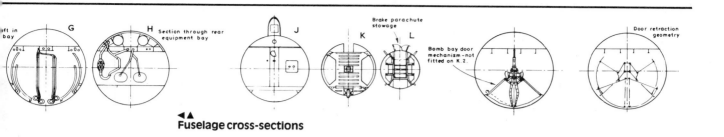

Section through rear equipment bay

Brake parachute stowage

Bomb bay door mechanism - not fitted on K.2.

Door retraction geometry

◄◄ **Fuselage cross-sections**

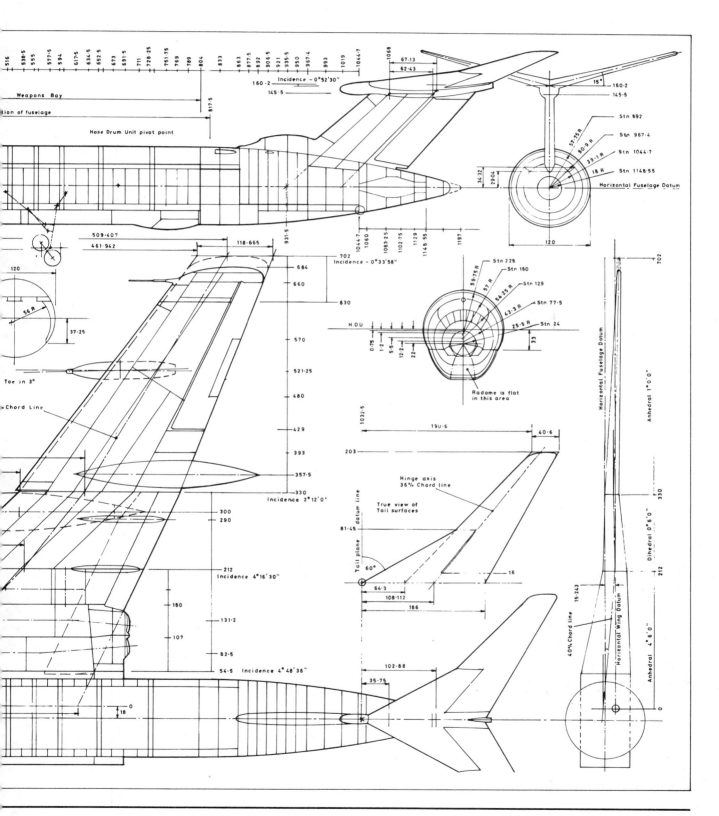

Dassault Mirage IIIC

Country of origin: France.
Type: Single-seat, land-based interceptor fighter.
Dimensions: Wing span 26ft 11½in *8.22m*; length (exc probe) 48ft 4¾in *14.75m*; height 13ft 11½in *4.25m*; wing area 377 sq ft *35.0m²*.
Weights: Empty equipped 13,555–13,995lb *6150–6350kg*; mission take-off

17,545–21,445lb *7960–9730kg*.
Powerplant: One SNECMA Atar 9B afterburning turbojet of 13,225lb *6000kg* maximum thrust.
Performance: Maximum speed Mach 2.15 at 36,100ft *11,000m*; initial climb rate over 16,400ft/min *5000m/min*; service ceiling 55,770ft *17,000m*; range (clean, at altitude) over 1000 miles *1600km*.

Armament: Two fixed 30mm DEFA 5-52 cannon, plus (optional) one Matra R.530 AAM and two AIM-9 Sidewinder or R.550 Magic AAMs, or up to 3000lb *1360kg* of bombs.
Service: First flight 9 October 1960; service entry October 1961.

DRAWN BY D H COOKSEY

O

Y. OUTLINE

K

M

Y & B DIAGONAL STRIPES

Underplan, IIIC
Starboard side
▼

2

NE PAS MARCHER

NE PAS MARCHER

L

B

NE PAS MARCHER

J

E

NE PAS MARCHER

5.

MG.

▲
Plan view, IIIC
Starboard side

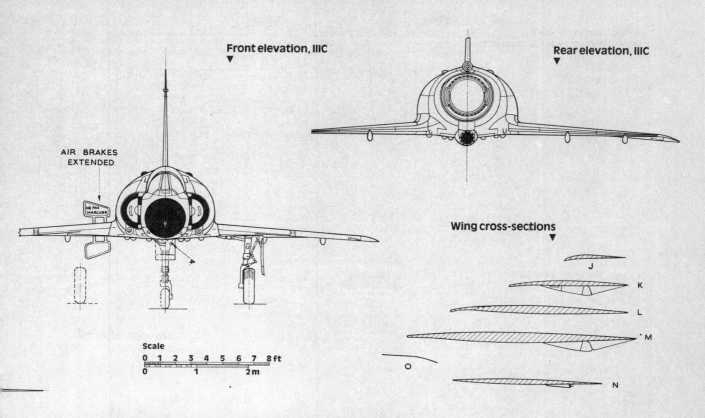

Front elevation, IIIC ▼

AIR BRAKES
EXTENDED

NE PAS
MARCHER

Rear elevation, IIIC ▼

Wing cross-sections ▼

J

K

L

M

O

N

Scale

0 1 2 3 4 5 6 7 8 ft

0   1   2 m

French fighter power in the 1960s: Mirage IIICs on the flight
line. The IIIC had formed the basis for one of the most
successful of all postwar military aircraft.
▼

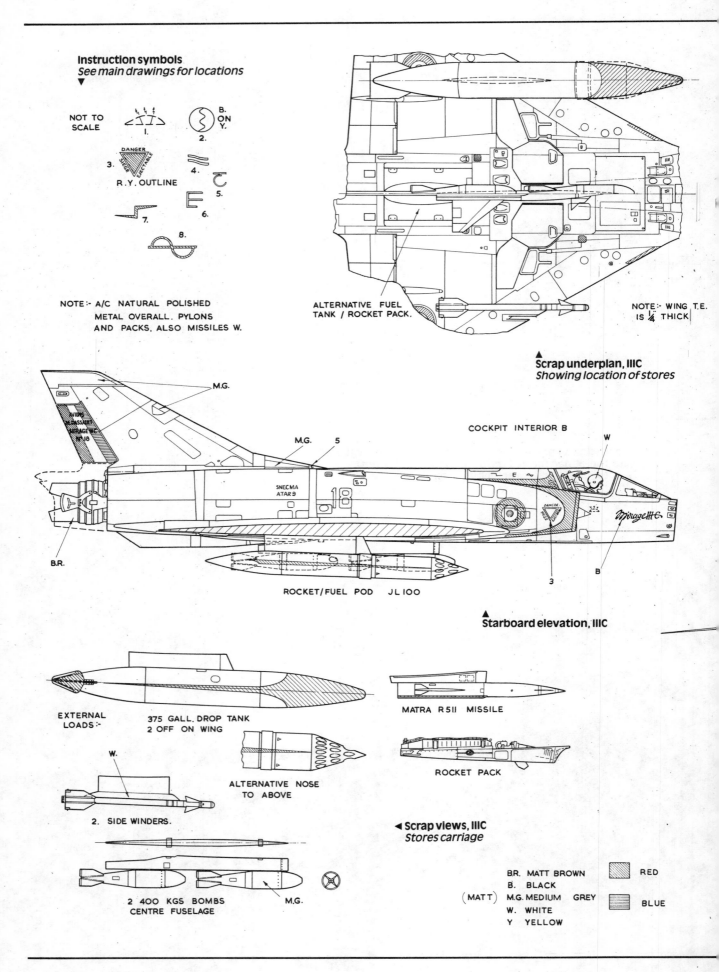

Instruction symbols
See main drawings for locations
▼

NOT TO SCALE

1.

2. B. ON Y.

3. DANGER SIEGE EJECTABLE

R.Y. OUTLINE

4.

5.

6.

7.

8.

NOTE:- A/C NATURAL POLISHED METAL OVERALL. PYLONS AND PACKS, ALSO MISSILES W.

ALTERNATIVE FUEL TANK / ROCKET PACK.

NOTE:- WING T.E. IS ¼ THICK

▲ **Scrap underplan, IIIC**
Showing location of stores

M.G.

AVIONS M. DASSAULT MIRAGE III C N° 18

M.G.

M.G. 5

SNECMA ATAR 9

COCKPIT INTERIOR B

W

B.R.

DANGER SIEGE EJECTABLE

Mirage III C

B

3

ROCKET/FUEL POD JL 100

▲ **Starboard elevation, IIIC**

EXTERNAL LOADS:-

375 GALL. DROP TANK 2 OFF ON WING

ALTERNATIVE NOSE TO ABOVE

MATRA R 511 MISSILE

ROCKET PACK

W.

2. SIDE WINDERS.

◀ **Scrap views, IIIC**
Stores carriage

2 400 KGS BOMBS CENTRE FUSELAGE

M.G.

(MATT) B.R. MATT BROWN
B. BLACK
M.G. MEDIUM GREY
W. WHITE
Y YELLOW

RED

BLUE

Scale

0 1 2 3 4 5 6 7 8 ft
0   1   2 m

▲
RAAF Mirage IIIO is one of many export variants of the Mirage III/V family. This one has a dramatic yellow high-visibility scheme.

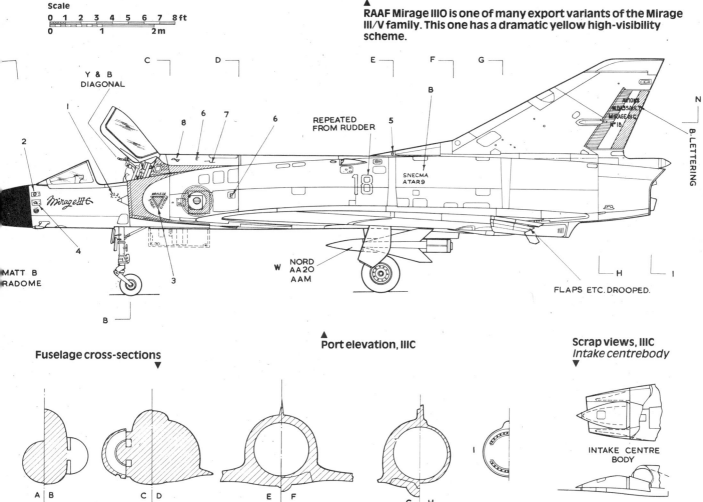

Y & B DIAGONAL

C   D   E   F   G

Z

B. LETTERING

I

8   6   7   6

REPEATED FROM RUDDER

B

SNECMA ATAR 9

5

AVIONS MARCEL DASSAULT MIRAGE III C No 18

2

Mirage III C

18

4

MATT B RADOME

3

B

W   NORD AA 20 AAM

H   I

FLAPS ETC. DROOPED.

▲
Port elevation, IIIC

Fuselage cross-sections
▼

A | B   C | D   E | F   G | H   I

Scrap views, IIIC
Intake centrebody
▼

INTAKE CENTRE BODY

BAC Lightning F Mk 6

Country of origin: Great Britain.
Type: Single-seat, land-based interceptor fighter.
Dimensions: Wing span 34ft 10in *10.62m*; length 55ft 3in *16.84m*; height 19ft 7in *5.97m*; wing area 380.1 sq ft *35.31m²*.
Weights: Empty about 28,000lb *12,700kg*;

loaded about 50,000lb *22,700kg*.
Powerplant: Two Rolls-Royce Avon 302 afterburning turbojets each of 15,680lb *7115kg* maximum thrust.
Performance: Maximum speed 1500mph *2415kph* at 40,000ft *12,200m*; initial climb rate 50,000ft/min *15,240m/min*; service ceiling 60,000ft *18,290m*; range 800 miles

1290km.
Armament: Two Red Top or Firestreak AAMs, plus (optional) two fixed 30mm Aden cannon in belly fairing; other weapons possible (see drawings).
Service: First flight (P.1A) 4 August 1954, (F Mk 6) 17 April 1964.

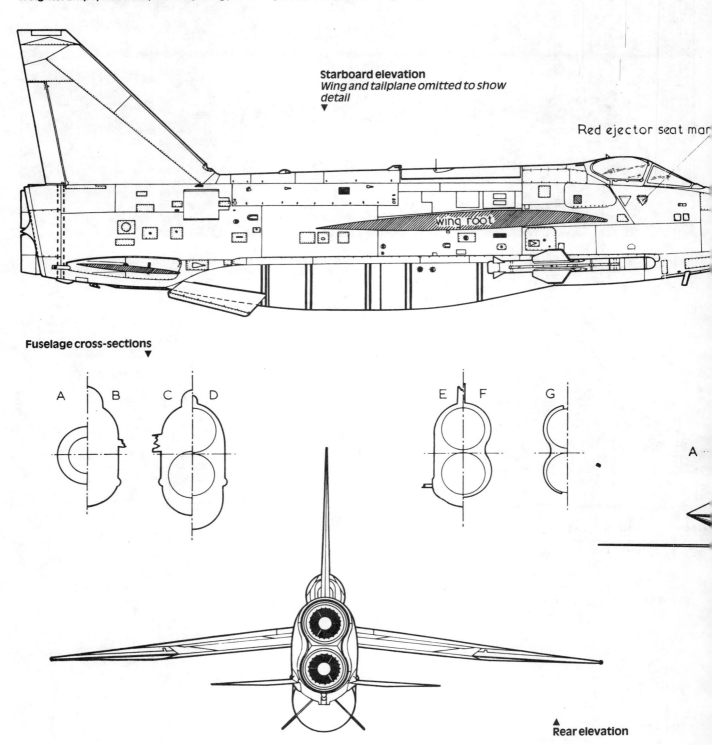

Starboard elevation
Wing and tailplane omitted to show detail
▼

Red ejector seat mar

wing root

Fuselage cross-sections
▼

A   B   C   D   E   F   G   A

Rear elevation
▲

66

▲
No 74(F) Squadron Lightning F.6 as depicted in the plans. Despite their limited range and ancient radar system, Lightnings still equipped two front-line RAF squadrons in 1987.

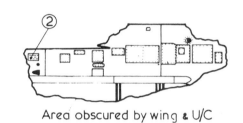

Area obscured by wing & U/C

Scale

0 1 2 3 4 5 6 7 8 ft

0   1   2 m

Matt black

B   C   D   E

H   H

Matt black
anti-glare
panel and
canopy

Yellow lines

①

XR773

Black on yellow
background

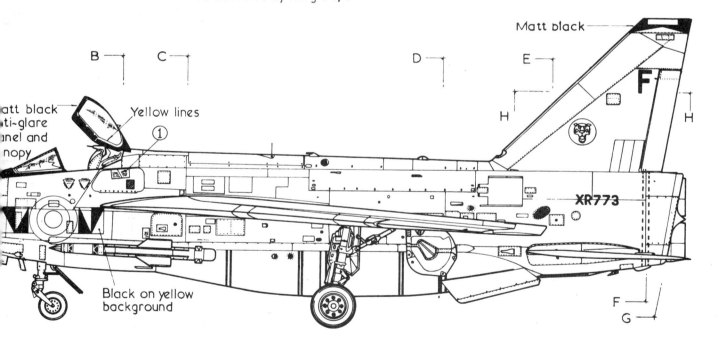

F
G

▲
Port elevation

Red

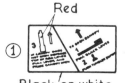

①

Black on white

| DANGER
STARTER
EXHAUST
KEEP CLEAR | ② |

Red on white

DRAWN BY C J NICHOLS

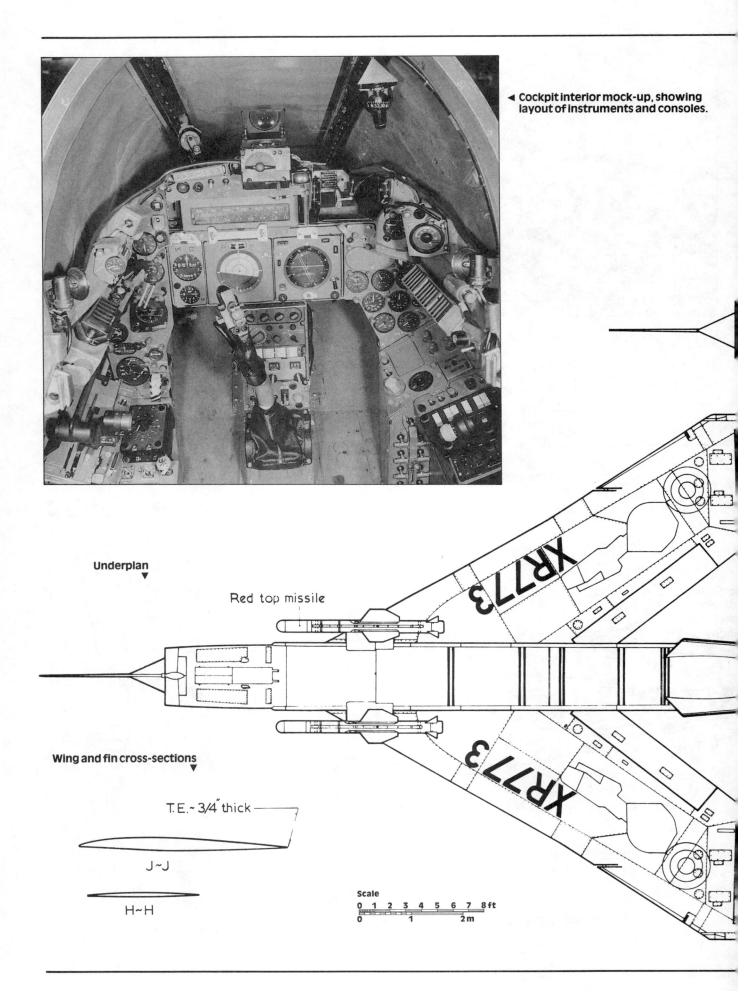

◄ Cockpit interior mock-up, showing layout of instruments and consoles.

Underplan
▼

Red top missile

Wing and fin cross-sections
▼

T.E.~ 3/4″ thick

J~J

H~H

XR773

XR773

Scale
0 1 2 3 4 5 6 7 8 ft
0   1   2 m

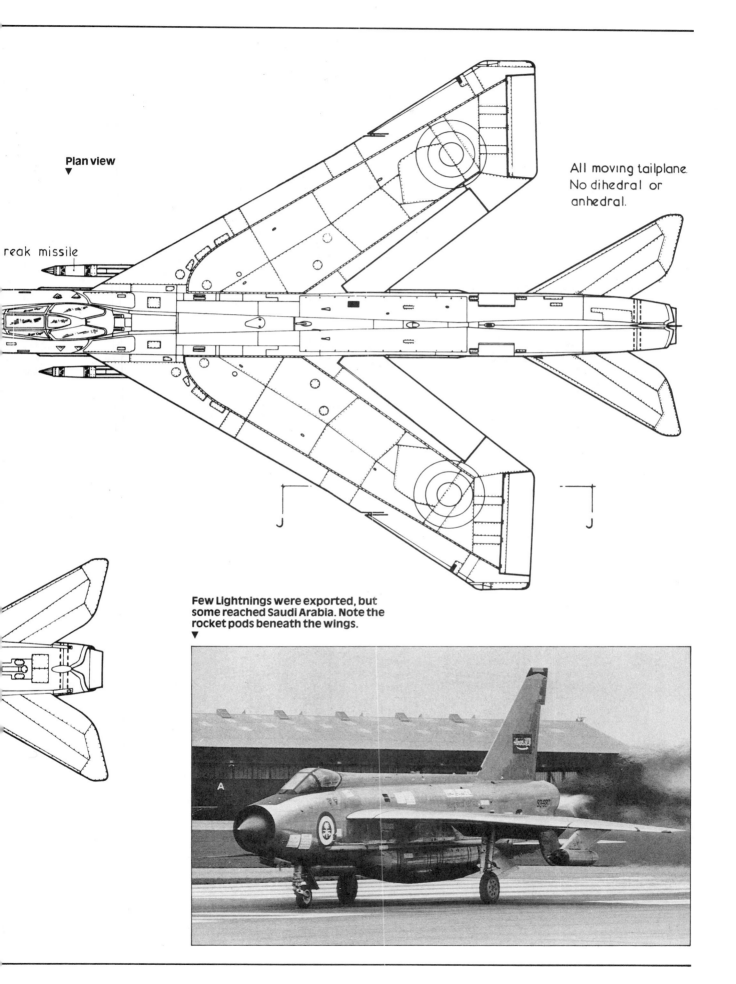

Plan view
▼

reak missile

All moving tailplane.
No dihedral or
anhedral.

J   J

**Few Lightnings were exported, but
some reached Saudi Arabia. Note the
rocket pods beneath the wings.**
▼

▲
Lightning F.6 with Red Top missiles and overwing tanks. The refuelling probe became standard fit.

Numerical key

1. 1000lb HE retarded or fire bomb. **2.** Matra 155. **3.** Matra 100. **4.** 260gal ferry tank. **5.** Twin Matra 155. **6.** Matra 155. **7.** Twin 1000lb or fire bombs. **8.** 1000lb bomb or fire bomb. **9.** Twin Aden gun pack, interchangeable with forward ventral fuel tank. **10.** Retractable glass-fibre rocket launchers (22 rockets per side), interchangeable with missile packs and reconnaissance pack. **11.** Reconnaissance pack. **12.** Daylight camera carrier, night camera carrier or line scan and camera carrier.

Front elevation ▶

Scale

0 1 2 3 4 5 6 7 8 ft

0   1   2 m

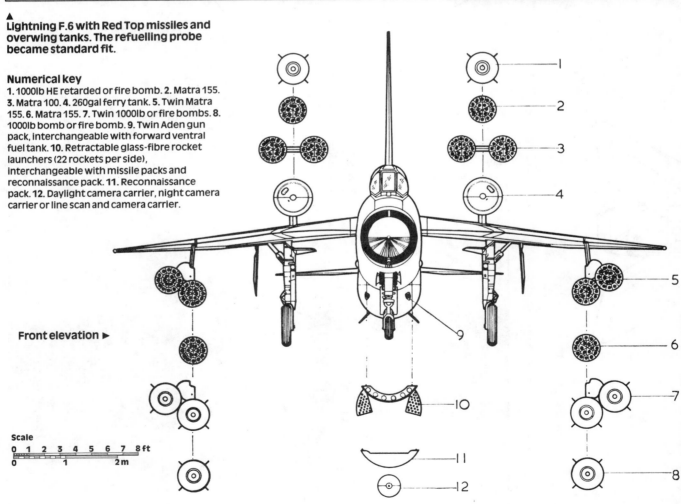

Hawker Siddeley Harrier GR Mk 1 and T Mk 2

Country of origin: Great Britain.
Type: Single-seat, land-based, V/STOL tactical attack and reconnaissance aircraft and (T Mk 2) two-seat trainer.
Dimensions: Wing span 25ft 3in *7.70m*; length 45ft 6in *13.87m*, (T Mk 2) 55ft 9½in *17.01m*; height 11ft 3in *3.43m*, (T Mk 2) 12ft 2in *3.71m*; wing area 201 sq ft *18.67m²*.

Weights: Basic operating weight 12,200lb *5535kg*, (T Mk 2) 13,000lb *5900kg*; maximum take-off 22,000lb *9980kg*.
Powerplant: One Rolls-Royce Pegasus Mk 101 vectored-thrust turbofan of 19,000lb *8620kg*.
Performance: Maximum speed 740mph *1190kph* (Mach 0.98); initial climb rate 50,000ft/min *15,240m/min*; service

ceiling over 50,000ft; range (ferry) 2070 miles *3330km*.
Armament: Two fixed 30mm Aden cannon in detachable pods; up to 8000lb *3630kg* external ordnance.
Service: First flight (P.1127) 21 October 1960, (GR Mk 1) 28 December 1967, (T Mk 2) 24 April 1969; service entry (GR Mk 1) April 1969.

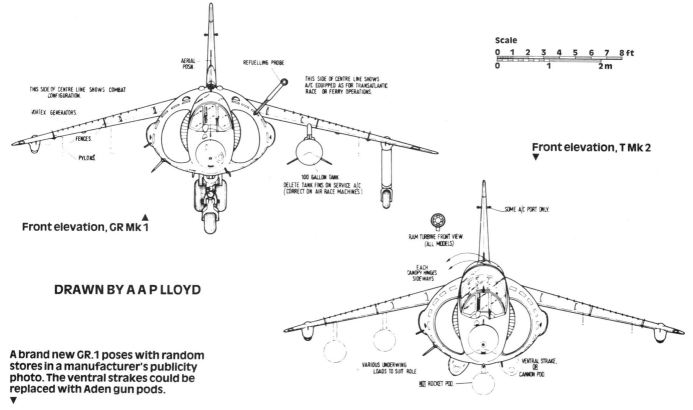

Front elevation, GR Mk 1 ▲

Front elevation, T Mk 2 ▼

DRAWN BY A A P LLOYD

A brand new GR.1 poses with random stores in a manufacturer's publicity photo. The ventral strakes could be replaced with Aden gun pods.
▼

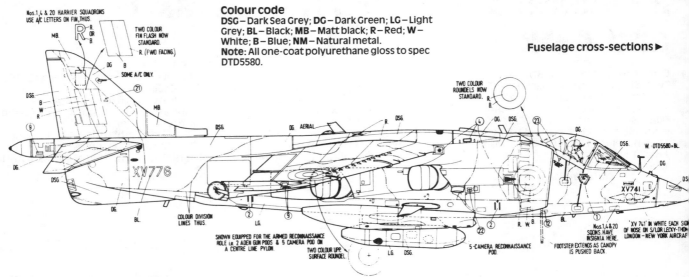

Colour code
DSG – Dark Sea Grey; **DG** – Dark Green; **LG** – Light Grey; **BL** – Black; **MB** – Matt black; **R** – Red; **W** – White; **B** – Blue; **NM** – Natural metal.
Note: All one-coat polyurethane gloss to spec DTD5580.

Nos.1,4 & 20 HARRIER SQUADRONS USE A/C LETTERS ON FIN, THUS.

TWO COLOUR FIN FLASH NOW STANDARD. R. (FWD FACING.)

SOME A/C ONLY.

TWO COLOUR ROUNDELS NOW STANDARD.

W. DTD5580 – BL.

XV776

XV741

'XV 741' IN WHITE EACH SIDE OF NOSE ON S/LDR LECKY-THOMPSON LONDON – NEW YORK AIRCRAFT

SHOWN EQUIPPED FOR THE ARMED RECONNAISSANCE ROLE i.e. 2 ADEN GUN PODS & 5 CAMERA POD ON A CENTRE LINE PYLON.

COLOUR DIVISION LINES THUS.

TWO COLOUR UPP. SURFACE ROUNDEL.

5-CAMERA RECONNAISSANCE POD.

Nos.1,4 & 20 SQDNS. HAVE INSIGNIA HERE.

FOOTSTEP EXTENDS AS CANOPY IS PUSHED BACK.

▲ Starboard elevation, GR Mk 1

Sporting No. 1(F) Squadron markings, a Harrier GR.1 hovers over its hideaway. Current GR.3s have bulbous laser noses and other refinements. ▼

Numerical key

1. 'Ejection seat' – R triangle, R and W lettering. 2. 'Trestle here' – BL arrow and lines. 3. 'Armament safety key – locked' – BL lettering, W aligning bars. 4. 'Fire access' – R bordered by 1in R outlines. 5. Crosses 8in × 1in R, panel edged 1in R line. 6. 'Wing trestle, not A/C jacking' – BL letters and tee. 7. Incidence degrees – BL 1in × ⅜in bars at 2° intervals +4° to –10°. 8. R 1in band round edge of fwd T/P aperture. 9. 'Danger Power control & jet blast' – R. 10. Normal canopy release. 11. 'Ensure

personnel are clear of footstep before releasing canopy' – BL. 12. 'Keep clear of footstep when canopy is released. Push in to lock canopy' – BL. 13. 'Emergency canopy release other side'. 14. Mic. Tel. – Y and BL symbol. 15. Hoisting point – Pale green and BL symbol. 16. Vector angles – 1¾in × ½in BL bars at 10° intervals from thrust line, 1in numbers at 0°, 30°, 60°, 90° and 98½°, port fwd nozzle only. 17. 'Earth. Fuel. Nitrogen. Engine oil' etc – BL on W panel. 18. 'Air brake lock'. 19. 'APU output'.

20. 'Electrical ground supply'. 21. 'Slinging point'. 22. 'Hydraulic fluid No 2 System – Defuelling pressure connection'. 23. Yellow dotted lines indicate where to break into canopy for rescue. 24. 'Water'. 25. 'Nitrogen'. 26. 'Danger – Keep clear'. 27. 'Danger – Explosive release' – in R triangle similar to ejection seat marking. 28. 'Starter inlet and exhaust'.
Note: Ringed numbers indicate positioning of descriptive matter.

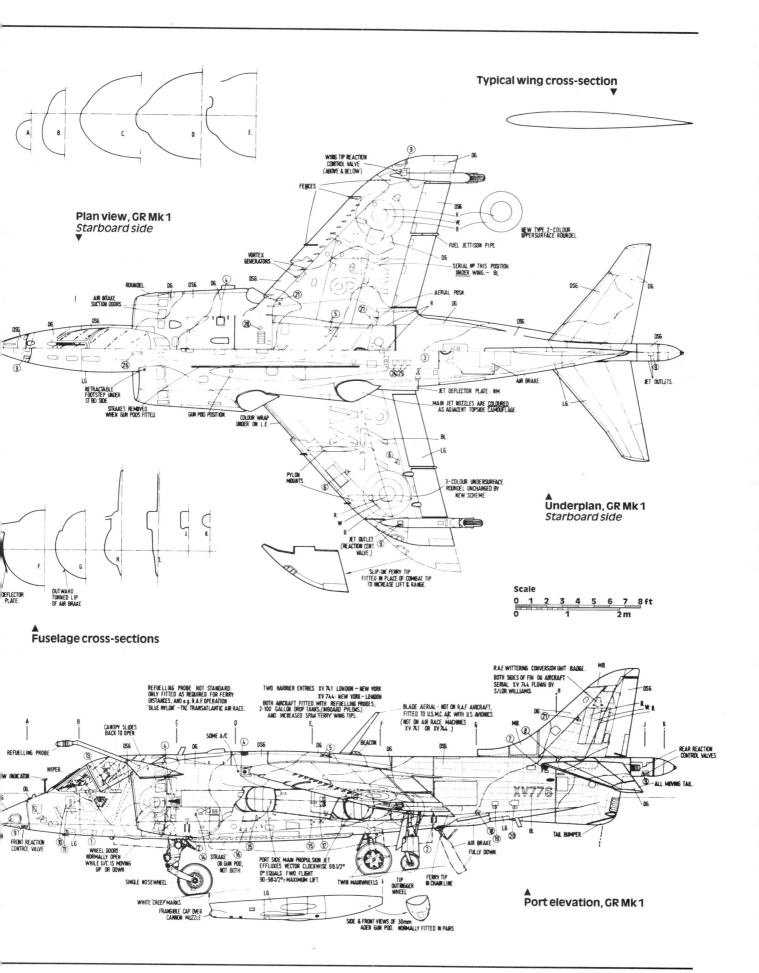

Typical wing cross-section

Plan view, GR Mk 1
Starboard side

WING TIP REACTION CONTROL VALVE (ABOVE & BELOW)

DG

FENCES

DSG
R
W
B

NEW TYPE 2-COLOUR UPPERSURFACE ROUNDEL.

FUEL JETTISON PIPE

DG

VORTEX GENERATORS

SERIAL Nº THIS POSITION UNDER WING.- BL.

ROUNDEL   DG   DSG   DG   DSG

AERIAL POSN.

AIR INTAKE SUCTION DOORS

R   DG

DSG   DG   DSG

DSG

DSG   DG   DSG

DSG

RETRACTABLE FOOTSTEP UNDER ST BD SIDE

STRAKES REMOVED WHEN GUN PODS FITTED.

GUN POD POSITION.

COLOUR 'WRAP UNDER' ON L.E.

AIR BRAKE

JET DEFLECTOR PLATE : NM

MAIN JET NOZZLES ARE COLOURED AS ADJACENT TOPSIDE CAMOUFLAGE.

JET OUTLETS.

L.G.

BL.

L.G.

PYLON MOUNTS.

3-COLOUR UNDERSURFACE ROUNDEL UNCHANGED BY NEW SCHEME.

Underplan, GR Mk 1
Starboard side

R
W
B

JET OUTLET (REACTION CONT. VALVE.)

'SLIP-ON' FERRY TIP FITTED IN PLACE OF COMBAT TIP TO INCREASE LIFT & RANGE.

Scale
0 1 2 3 4 5 6 7 8 ft
0   1   2 m

DEFLECTOR PLATE.

OUTWARD TURNED LIP OF AIR BRAKE.

Fuselage cross-sections

R.A.F. WITTERING CONVERSION UNIT BADGE. BOTH SIDES OF FIN ON AIRCRAFT SERIAL XV 744 FLOWN BY S/LDR WILLIAMS.

MB

DSG

REFUELLING PROBE NOT STANDARD: ONLY FITTED AS REQUIRED FOR FERRY DISTANCES, AND e.g. R.A.F. OPERATION 'BLUE NYLON'-THE TRANSATLANTIC AIR RACE.

TWO HARRIER ENTRIES XV 741: LONDON – NEW YORK
XV 744: NEW YORK – LONDON
BOTH AIRCRAFT FITTED WITH REFUELLING PROBES,
2-100 GALLON DROP TANKS, (INBOARD PYLONS.)
AND INCREASED SPAN 'FERRY' WING TIPS.

BLADE AERIAL : NOT ON R.A.F AIRCRAFT, FITTED TO U.S.M.C. A/C WITH U.S. AVIONICS. (NOT ON AIR RACE MACHINES XV 741 OR XV 744.)

MB

R W B

CANOPY SLIDES BACK TO OPEN.

DSG

SOME A/C

DG   DSG   DG   DSG   DG   DSG

DG

REAR REACTION CONTROL VALVES.

REFUELLING PROBE

BEACON

DSG

DG

W INDICATOR.   WIPER

DG

ALL MOVING TAIL.

FRONT REACTION CONTROL VALVE.

WHEEL DOORS NORMALLY OPEN WHILE U/C IS MOVING UP OR DOWN

L.G.

STRAKE' OR GUN POD, NOT BOTH.

AIR BRAKE FULLY DOWN.

TAIL BUMPER.

L.G.   BL.

XV776

SINGLE NOSEWHEEL

PORT SIDE MAIN PROPULSION JET EFFLUXES VECTOR CLOCKWISE 98.1/2° 0° EQUALS FWD. FLIGHT 90-98.1/2°= MAXIMUM LIFT.

TWIN MAINWHEELS

TIP OUTRIGGER WHEEL

FERRY TIP IN CHAIN LINE

WHITE 'CREEP' MARKS.

FRANGIBLE CAP OVER CANNON MUZZLE.

L.G.

SIDE & FRONT VIEWS OF 30mm ADEN GUN POD. NORMALLY FITTED IN PAIRS.

Port elevation, GR Mk 1

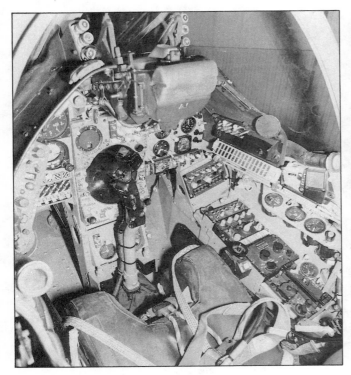

◀▲ Cockpit views – compare with drawing opposite. The close-in photo shows part of the rear cockpit of the T.60 (similar to T.2).

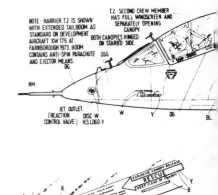

NOTE : HARRIER T 2 IS SHOWN WITH EXTENDED TAILBOOM AS STANDARD ON DEVELOPMENT AIRCRAFT XW 175 AT FARNBOROUGH 1973. BOOM CONTAINS ANTI-SPIN PARACHUTE AND EJECTOR MEANS. OG.

T.2 SECOND CREW MEMBER HAS FULL WINDSCREEN AND SEPARATELY OPENING CANOPY. BOTH CANOPIES HINGED ON STARB'D SIDE

DSG

NM.

JET OUTLET. (REACTION CONTROL VALVE.) DISC. W. H.S.LOGO. Y

W   Y   OG.   BL.

EXPLOSIVE CANOPY RELEASE

RESCUE
KEEP CLEAR OF CANOPY

ENLARGED PORT SIDE CANOPY RAIL. INDICATES PLACE & METHOD FOR OUTSIDE RESCUE

◀ T.2 take-off. Note long 'sting' at tail, to counterbalance the extension of the forward fuselage in the trainer version.

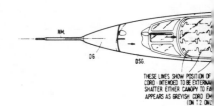

NM.

OG.   DSG.

THESE LINES SHOW POSITION OF CORD : INTENDED TO BE EXTERNAL SHATTER EITHER CANOPY TO FA APPEARS AS GREYISH CORD EM (ON T 2 ONL

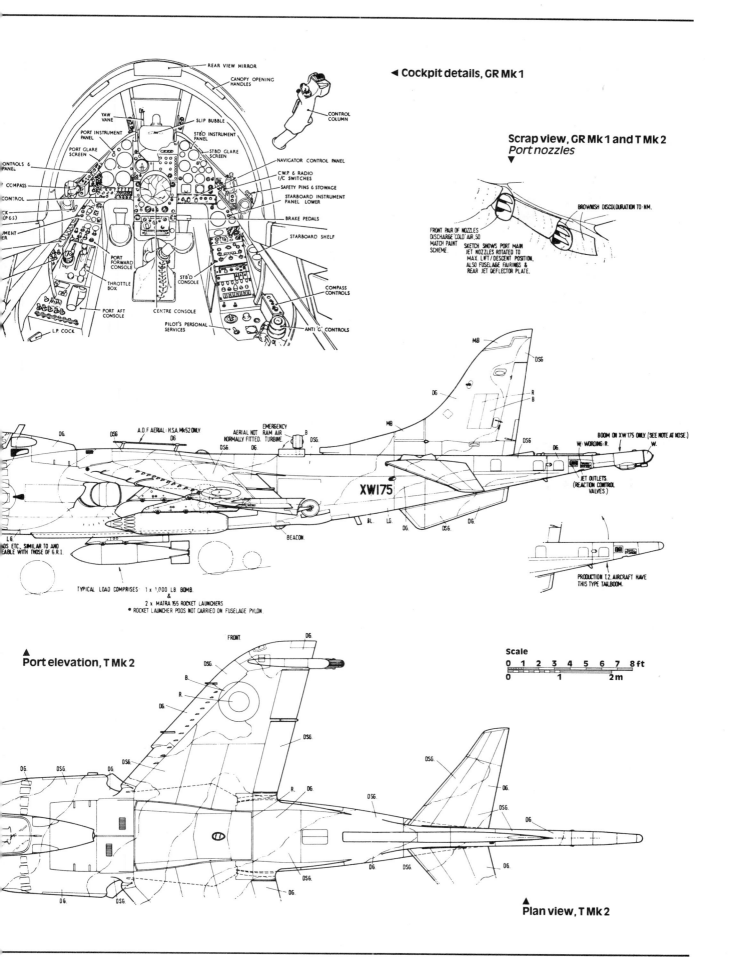

◄ Cockpit details, GR Mk 1

REAR VIEW MIRROR
CANOPY OPENING HANDLES
YAW VANE
SLIP BUBBLE
CONTROL COLUMN
PORT INSTRUMENT PANEL
STB'D INSTRUMENT PANEL
PORT GLARE SCREEN
STB'D GLARE SCREEN
CONTROLS &
PANEL
NAVIGATOR CONTROL PANEL
C.W.P. & RADIO I/C SWITCHES
COMPASS
CONTROL
SAFETY PINS & STOWAGE
STARBOARD INSTRUMENT PANEL LOWER
CK (P&S)
MENT
ER
BRAKE PEDALS
STARBOARD SHELF
PORT FORWARD CONSOLE
THROTTLE BOX
STB'D CONSOLE
COMPASS CONTROLS
PORT AFT CONSOLE
CENTRE CONSOLE
PILOT'S PERSONAL SERVICES
ANTI 'G' CONTROLS
L.P. COCK

Scrap view, GR Mk 1 and T Mk 2
Port nozzles
▼

FRONT PAIR OF NOZZLES DISCHARGE 'COLD' AIR, SO MATCH PAINT SCHEME
SKETCH SHOWS PORT MAIN JET NOZZLES ROTATED TO MAX. LIFT/DESCENT POSITION. ALSO FUSELAGE FAIRINGS & REAR JET DEFLECTOR PLATE.
BROWNISH DISCOLOURATION TO NM.

MB
DSG
DG
R
B
MB
DSG
DG
DG
DSG

A.D.F AERIAL: H.S.A. Mk 52 ONLY.
DG
AERIAL NOT NORMALLY FITTED.
EMERGENCY RAM AIR TURBINE.
B
DSG.
DG.
DSG.

BOOM ON XW 175 ONLY. (SEE NOTE AT NOSE.)
W: WORDING: R.
W.

JET OUTLETS (REACTION CONTROL VALVES.)

XW175

DS ETC. SIMILAR TO AND
EABLE WITH THOSE OF G.R.1.
L G.
BEACON.
BL.
LG.
DG.
DSG.
DG.

PRODUCTION T.2. AIRCRAFT HAVE THIS TYPE TAILBOOM.

TYPICAL LOAD COMPRISES: 1 x 1,000 LB BOMB.
&
2 x MATRA 155 ROCKET LAUNCHERS
* ROCKET LAUNCHER PODS NOT CARRIED ON FUSELAGE PYLON.

FRONT
DG.
DSG
B.
R.
DG
DSG

▲
Port elevation, T Mk 2

Scale
0 1 2 3 4 5 6 7 8 ft
0   1   2 m

DSG.
DG
DSG.
DSG.
DG.
DG.
DSG.
DSG.
DG
R.
DG
DSG.
DSG.
DG
DSG.
DG.
DSG.
DG.
DG
DSG.
DG.
DG.

▲
Plan view, T Mk 2

▲ US Marine Corps AV-8As were broadly similar to the GR.1 but, externally, had a prominent dorsal antenna. These two are from VMA-231.

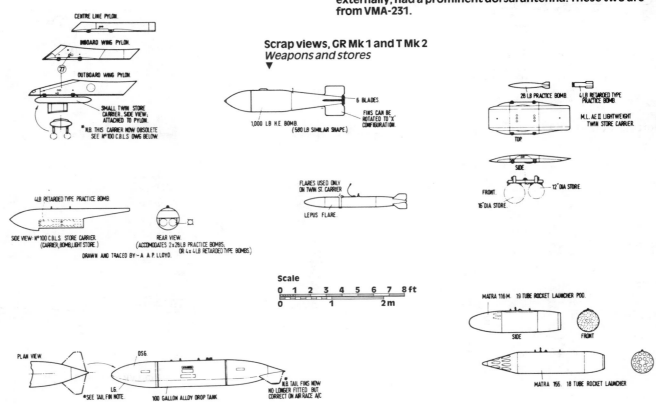

CENTRE LINE PYLON.

INBOARD WING PYLON.

(27)

OUTBOARD WING PYLON.

SMALL TWIN STORE CARRIER. SIDE VIEW: ATTACHED TO PYLON.

N.B. THIS CARRIER NOW OBSOLETE SEE Nº100 C.B.L.S DWG BELOW.

Scrap views, GR Mk 1 and T Mk 2
Weapons and stores
▼

6 BLADES.

FINS CAN BE ROTATED TO 'X' CONFIGURATION.

1,000 LB H.E. BOMB.
(580 LB SIMILAR SHAPE.)

28 LB PRACTICE BOMB.   4 LB RETARDED TYPE PRACTICE BOMB.

M.L. AE II LIGHTWEIGHT TWIN STORE CARRIER.

TOP

SIDE

FRONT   12" DIA STORE.

16" DIA STORE.

4 LB RETARDED TYPE PRACTICE BOMB.

FLARES USED ONLY ON TWIN ST. CARRIER.

LEPUS FLARE.

SIDE VIEW: Nº100 C.B.L.S STORE CARRIER.
(CARRIER, BOMB, LIGHT STORE.)

REAR VIEW.
(ACCOMMODATES 2 x 28 LB PRACTICE BOMBS;
OR 4 x 4 LB RETARDED TYPE BOMBS.)

DRAWN AND TRACED BY:- A A.P. LLOYD.

Scale

0 1 2 3 4 5 6 7 8 ft
0   1   2 m

MATRA 116 M. 19 TUBE ROCKET LAUNCHER POD.

SIDE   FRONT

MATRA 155. 18 TUBE ROCKET LAUNCHER.

PLAN VIEW   DSG.

*SEE TAIL FIN NOTE.   LG.   100 GALLON ALLOY DROP TANK.   N.B. TAIL FINS NOW NO LONGER FITTED BUT CORRECT ON AIR RACE A/C

SEPECAT Jaguar A, S, E, B and M

Countries of origin: France and Great Britain.
Type: Single-seat, land-based tactical attack aircraft and (B, E) two-seat trainer; (M) prototype single-seat, carrier-based tactical attack aircraft.
Dimensions: Wing span 27ft 10¼in *8.49m*; length 50ft 11in *15.52m*, (B, E) 53ft 11in *16.42m*; height 15ft 1½in *4.64m*; wing area 258.33 sq ft *24.00m²*.

Weights: Normal take-off 22,040lb *10,000kg*; maximum 30,865lb *14,000kg*.
Powerplant: Two Rolls-Royce/Turboméca RT172 Adour 102 augmented turbofans each of 7305lb *3315kg* thrust.
Performance: Maximum speed 1120mph *1800kph* (Mach 1.7) at 36,100ft *11,000m*; time to 30,000ft *9145m*, 2.5min; service ceiling 46,000ft *14,000m*; range (external fuel) 2800 miles *4500km*.

Armament: Two fixed 30mm DEFA cannon, (S) two fixed 30mm Aden cannon, (B) one fixed 30mm Aden cannon; up to 9900lb *4500kg* of external ordnance.
Service: First flight (prototype) 8 September 1968; service entry (A, E) May 1972, (S/GR Mk 1, B/T Mk 2) June 1973.

Scale
0 1 2 3 4 5 6 7 8 ft
0 1 2 m

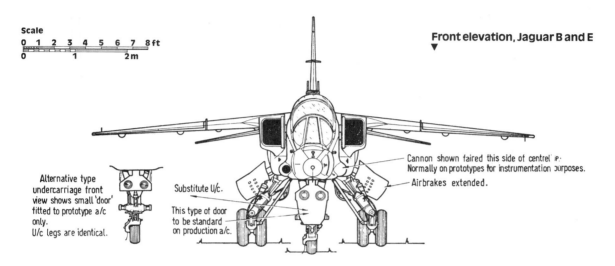

Front elevation, Jaguar B and E
▼

Cannon shown faired this side of centre line. Normally on prototypes for instrumentation purposes.
Airbrakes extended.

Alternative type undercarriage front view shows small 'door' fitted to prototype a/c only.
U/c legs are identical.

Substitute U/c.

This type of door to be standard on production a/c.

Prototype Jaguar E, French two-seater, shows original intake splitter plates and early-style nose gear door.
▼

Port elevation, Jaguar B and E ▼

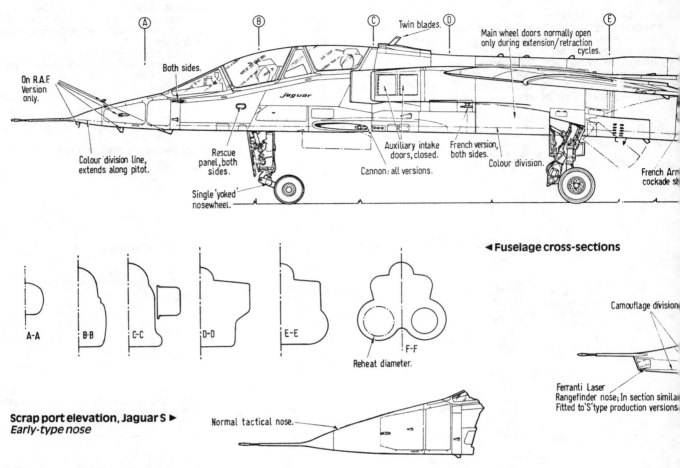

Ⓐ Ⓑ Ⓒ Twin blades. Ⓓ Main wheel doors normally open only during extension/retraction cycles. Ⓔ

Both sides.

On R.A.F Version only.

Colour division line, extends along pitot.

Rescue panel, both sides.

Single 'yoked' nosewheel.

Auxiliary intake doors, closed.

Cannon: all versions.

French version, both sides.

Colour division.

French Arm cockade sh

◄ **Fuselage cross-sections**

A-A   B-B   C-C   D-D   E-E   F-F

Reheat diameter.

Camouflage division

Ferranti Laser Rangefinder nose; In section similar Fitted to 'S' type production versions.

Scrap port elevation, Jaguar S ► *Early-type nose*

Normal tactical nose.

S06 during flight trials, with pre-production nose shape and low fin. ▼

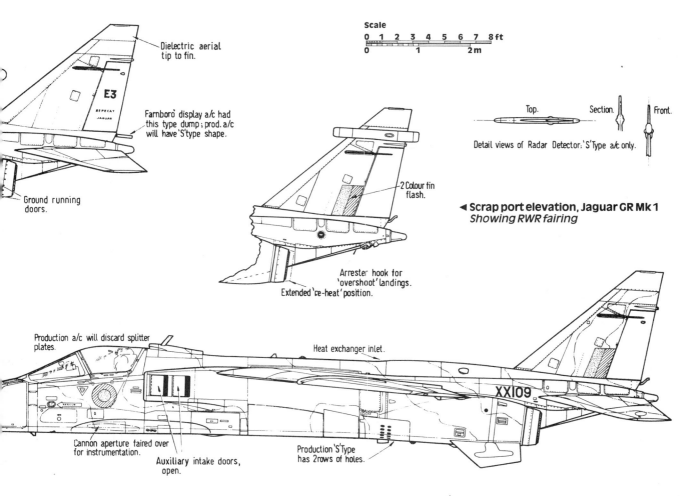

Dielectric aerial tip to fin.

E3

SEPECAT JAGUAR

Ground running doors.

Farnboro' display a/c had this type dump; prod. a/c will have 'S'type shape.

Scale
0 1 2 3 4 5 6 7 8 ft
0 1 2 m

Top. Section. Front.

Detail views of Radar Detector. 'S'Type a/c only.

2 Colour fin flash.

◄ **Scrap port elevation, Jaguar GR Mk 1**
Showing RWR fairing

Arrester hook for 'overshoot' landings.
Extended 're-heat' position.

Production a/c will discard splitter plates.

Heat exchanger inlet.

XX109

Cannon aperture faired over for instrumentation.

Auxiliary intake doors, open.

Production 'S'Type has 2 rows of holes.

▲
Port elevation, Jaguar GR Mk 1

E01 again. Two-seat Jaguars have a strike capability – they are far too expensive to use as mere trainers!
▼

Colour code
1. 'Rescue' arrow – yellow outlined black. **2.** Ejection seat triangle – red outlined white. **3.** 'Danger air intake keep clear' – black and white bars. **4.** 'Cut here emergency', canopy edge dotted 'break in' line and letters – yellow. **5.** Fire access panels edged with stripes – red. **Note:** Prototypes and pre-production aircraft varied in detail.

R.A.F. Version

▲
Early-production Jaguar GR Mk 1 showing chisel-shaped laser nose. Starboard spoiler is raised, enabling the aircraft to roll, and slats are extended.

Starboard elevation, Jaguar S06
▼

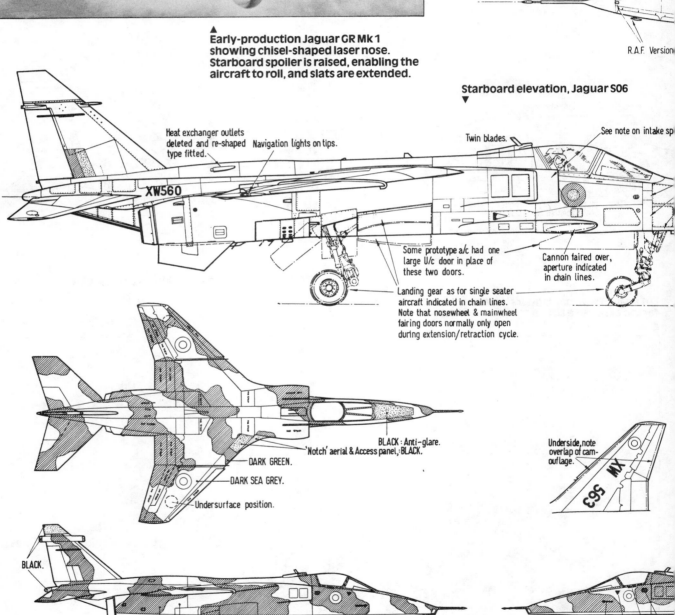

Heat exchanger outlets deleted and re-shaped type fitted.

Navigation lights on tips.

Twin blades.

See note on intake sp

XW560

Some prototype a/c had one large U/c door in place of these two doors.

Cannon faired over, aperture indicated in chain lines.

Landing gear as for single seater aircraft indicated in chain lines. Note that nosewheel & mainwheel fairing doors normally only open during extension/retraction cycle.

BLACK : Anti-glare.
'Notch' aerial & Access panel, BLACK.

DARK GREEN.

DARK SEA GREY.

Undersurface position.

Underside, note overlap of cam-ouflage.

XW 563

BLACK.

DARK SEA GREY. LIGHT GREY

DARK GREEN.

1

2   4   3

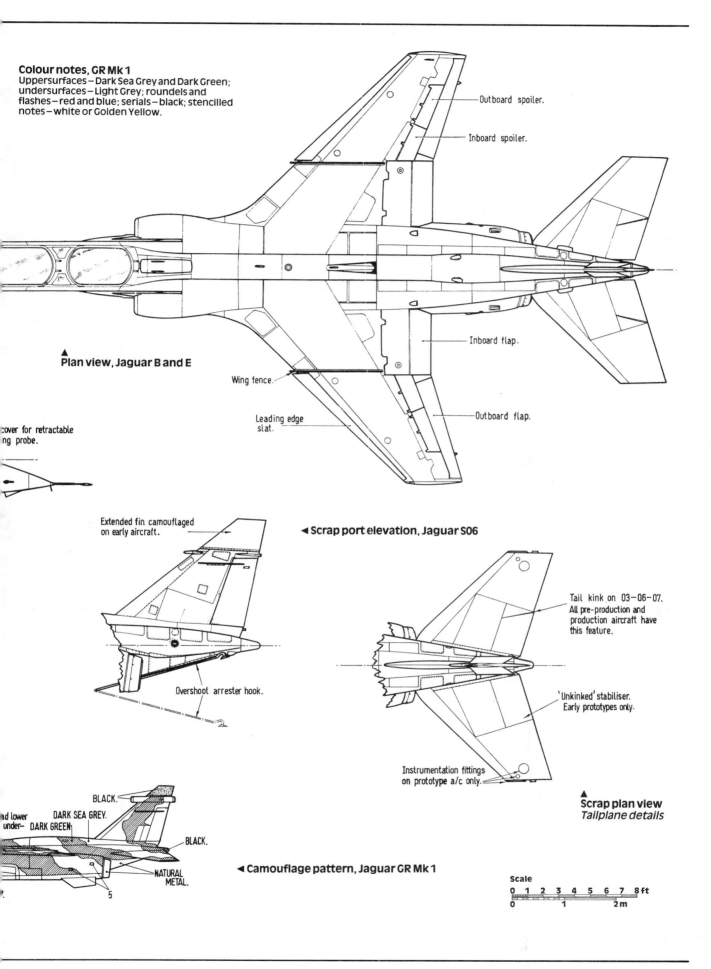

Colour notes, GR Mk 1
Uppersurfaces – Dark Sea Grey and Dark Green;
undersurfaces – Light Grey; roundels and
flashes – red and blue; serials – black; stencilled
notes – white or Golden Yellow.

Outboard spoiler.

Inboard spoiler.

Inboard flap.

▲
Plan view, Jaguar B and E

Wing fence.

Leading edge
slat.

Outboard flap.

cover for retractable
ng probe.

Extended fin camouflaged
on early aircraft.

◄ Scrap port elevation, Jaguar S06

Tail kink on 03–06–07.
All pre-production and
production aircraft have
this feature.

Overshoot arrester hook.

'Unkinked' stabiliser.
Early prototypes only.

Instrumentation fittings
on prototype a/c only.

▲
Scrap plan view
Tailplane details

BLACK.

d lower
under- DARK SEA GREY.
DARK GREEN

BLACK.

NATURAL
METAL.

5

◄ Camouflage pattern, Jaguar GR Mk 1

Scale
0 1 2 3 4 5 6 7 8 ft
0   1   2 m

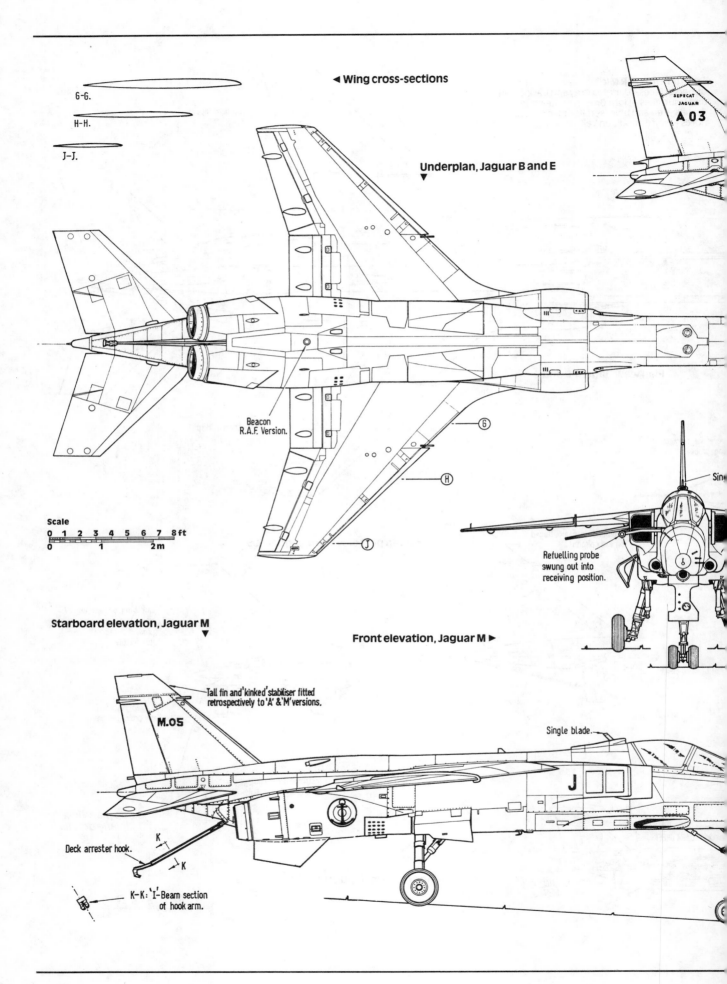

◄ **Wing cross-sections**

G-G.

H-H.

J-J.

Underplan, Jaguar B and E
▼

SEPECAT
JAGUAR

A 03

Beacon
R.A.F. Version.

G

H

J

Scale

0 1 2 3 4 5 6 7 8 ft

0   1   2 m

Sin

Refuelling probe
swung out into
receiving position.

Starboard elevation, Jaguar M
▼

Front elevation, Jaguar M ►

Tall fin and 'kinked' stabiliser fitted
retrospectively to 'A' & 'M' versions.

M.05

Single blade.

J

Deck arrester hook.

K

K

K–K: 'I'-Beam section
of hook arm.

Starboard elevation, Jaguar A03
▼

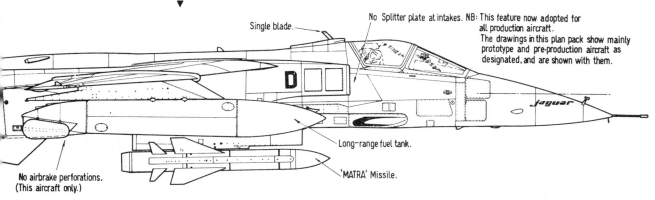

Single blade.

No Splitter plate at intakes. NB: This feature now adopted for all production aircraft.
The drawings in this plan pack show mainly prototype and pre-production aircraft as designated, and are shown with them.

D

Long-range fuel tank.

'MATRA' Missile.

No airbrake perforations. (This aircraft only.)

DRAWN BY C J NICHOLS AND A A P LLOYD

R.A.F. Version only.

fences.

levation: type 'M', arriage differs on ersions. : See sheet 2.

▲
Export two-seater for the Sultan of Oman's Air Force.

The navalised Jaguar M, a programme abandoned in favour of the Super Etendard.
▼

uelling probe in tended position.

d noseleg on maritime equipped with twin eels.

Grumman F-14A Tomcat

Country of origin: USA.
Type: Two-seat, carrier-based, multi-role fighter.
Dimensions: Wing span (maximum sweep) 38ft 2in *11.63m*, (minimum sweep) 64ft 1½in *19.54m*; length 62ft 8in *19.10m*; height 16ft 0in *4.88m*; wing area 565 sq ft *52.49m²*.
Weights: Empty 40,104lb *18,191kg*;

normal loaded 58,539lb *26,552kg*; maximum loaded 74,348lb *33,724kg*.
Powerplant: Two Pratt & Whitney TF30-412A two-shaft, afterburning turbofans each of 20,900lb *9480kg* thrust.
Performance: Maximum speed 1544mph *2485kph* (Mach 2.34); initial climb rate (normal loaded) 30,000ft/min *9150m/min*; range (external fuel) 2000 miles

3220km.
Armament: One fixed 20mm M61A1 cannon; four AIM-7 plus four or eight AIM-9 AAMs, or up to six AIM-54 AAMs plus two AIM-9 AAMs; (attack role) up to 14,500lb *6580kg* of ordnance.
Service: First flight (prototype) 21 December 1971; service entry 31 December 1972.

▲ F-14A with a full complement of AIM-54 Phoenix missiles and wings at maximum sweep.

◄ Tomcat front cockpit.

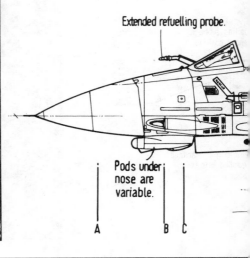

Extended refuelling probe.

Pods under nose are variable.

A   B C

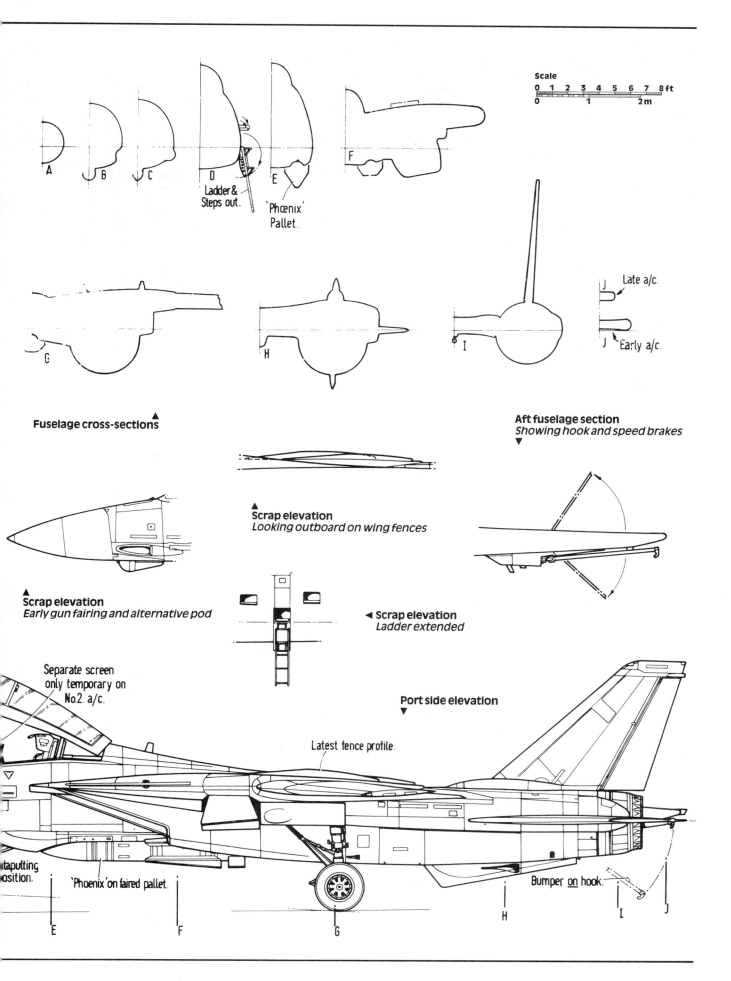

Scale

A B C D

Ladder & Steps out.

'Phœnix' Pallet.

E F

G H I

J — Late a/c.

J — Early a/c.

Fuselage cross-sections ▲

Aft fuselage section
Showing hook and speed brakes ▼

▲
Scrap elevation
Looking outboard on wing fences

▲
Scrap elevation
Early gun fairing and alternative pod

◄ **Scrap elevation**
Ladder extended

Port side elevation ▼

Separate screen only temporary on No.2. a/c.

Latest fence profile.

...tapulting ...osition.

'Phœnix' on faired pallet.

Bumper on hook.

E F G H I J

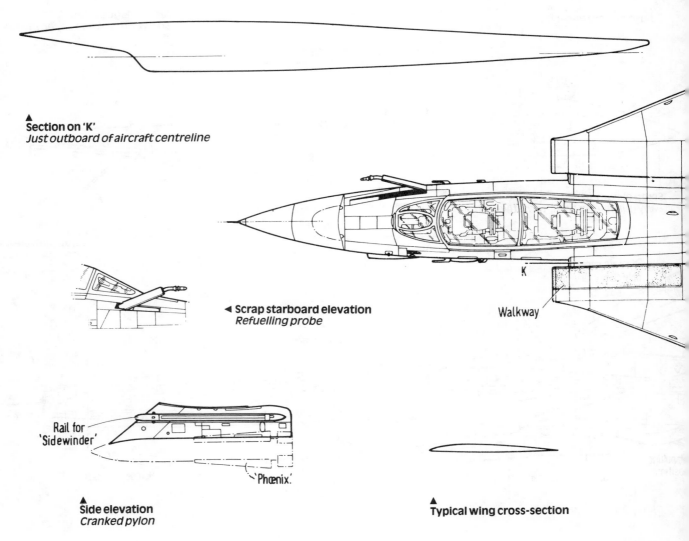

▲ **Section on 'K'**
Just outboard of aircraft centreline

◀ **Scrap starboard elevation**
Refuelling probe

Walkway

K

Rail for
'Sidewinder'

'Phœnix.'

▲ **Side elevation**
Cranked pylon

▲ **Typical wing cross-section**

◄ Unarmed F-14A from VF-84 'Jolly Rogers', with black, white and yellow tail decor. Although primarily an air-to-air fighter, the Tomcat can, if required, lift seven tons of air-to-ground ordnance in the strike role.

Scale

0 1 2 3 4 5 6 7 8 ft

0 1 2 m

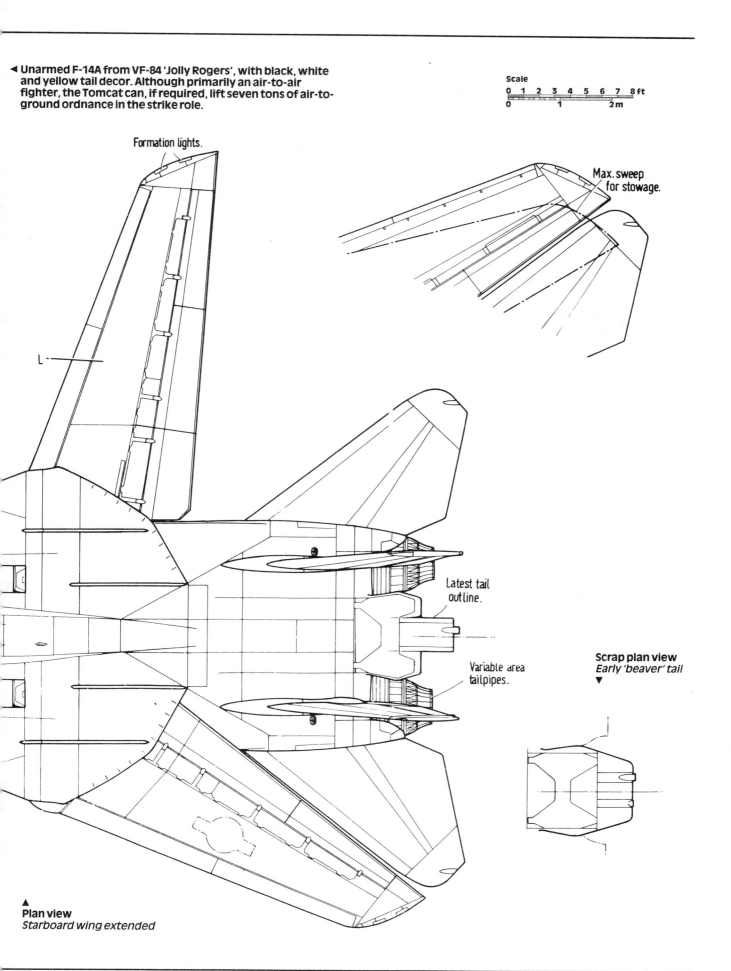

Formation lights.

Max. sweep for stowage.

L

Latest tail outline.

Variable area tailpipes.

Scrap plan view
Early 'beaver' tail
▼

▲
Plan view
Starboard wing extended

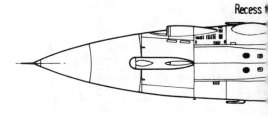

Recess

◀ Tail details of a VF-143 machine. Markings on US Navy aircraft are strictly 'low-viz' these days!

'Phœnix' lines: 2 each sid

Scale
0 1 2 3 4 5 6 7 8 ft
0 1 2 m

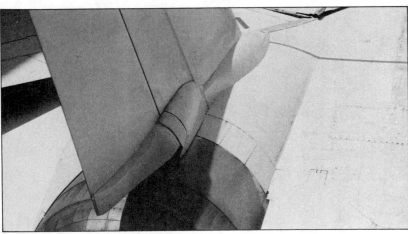

▲ Close-up photo showing details of fairings around base of port fin.

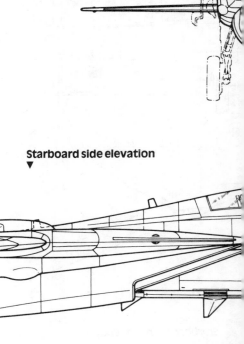

Starboard side elevation
▼

NOTE: Single formation light each outer fin tip. (A/C Nº 39 on.)

E.C.M Pod, st'bd fin tip.

NOTE: This elevation shows early type fences, and arrester hook.

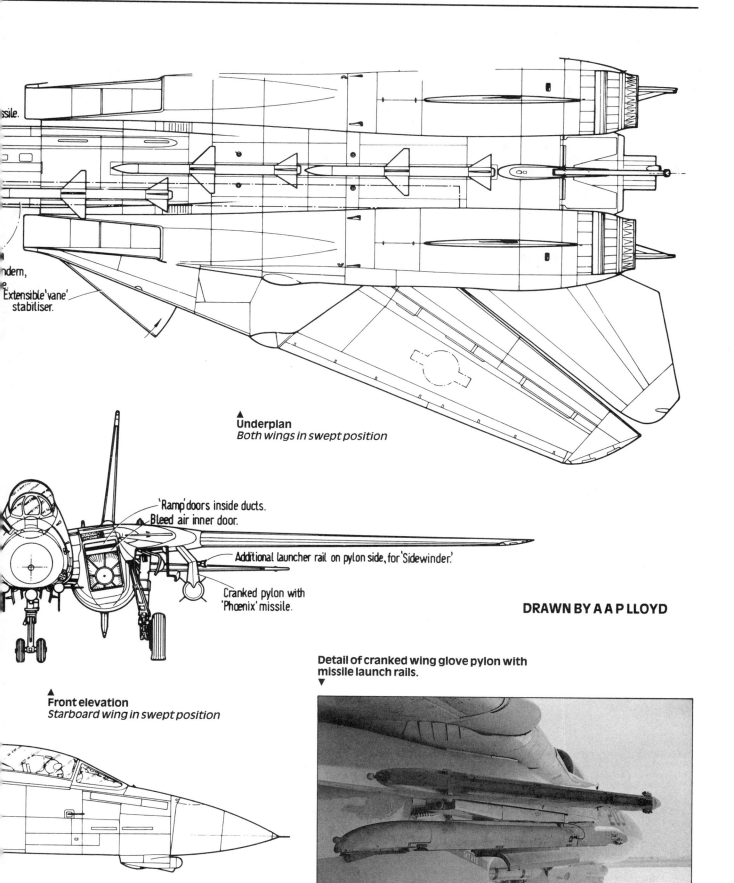

ssile.

ndem,
e
'Extensible 'vane'
stabiliser.

▲ **Underplan**
Both wings in swept position

'Ramp'doors inside ducts.
Bleed air inner door.

Additional launcher rail on pylon side, for 'Sidewinder.'

Cranked pylon with
'Phoenix' missile.

DRAWN BY A A P LLOYD

▲ **Front elevation**
Starboard wing in swept position

Detail of cranked wing glove pylon with
missile launch rails.
▼

Panavia Tornado GR Mk 1

Countries of origin: Great Britain, West Germany and Italy.
Type: Two-seat, land-based, multi-role strike aircraft.
Dimensions: Wing span (maximum sweep) 28ft 2½in *8.60m*, (minimum sweep) 45ft 7½in *13.91m*; length 54ft 10¼in *16.72m*; height 19ft 6¼in *5.95m*.
Weights: Empty equipped 31,065lb *14,095kg*; take-off (clean) 45,000lb

20,420kg; take-off (maximum) about 60,000lb *27,225kg*.
Powerplant: Two Turbo-Union RB199-34R Mk 101 augmented turbofans each of over 16,000lb *7260kg* maximum thrust.
Performance: Maximum speed (clean) over 1450mph *2335kph* (Mach 2.2) at altitude, over 920mph *1480kph* (Mach 1.2) at sea level; time to 30,0000ft *9150m* from brakes release, under 2min; service

ceiling over 50,000ft *15,250m*; range (ferry) about 2400 miles *3850km*.
Armament: Two fixed 27mm IWKA Mauser cannon, plus up to 18,000lb *8165kg* of external ordnance.
Service: First flight (prototype) 14 August 1974, (GR Mk 1) July 1979; service entry 6 January 1982.

Colour code
DSG – Dark Sea Grey; **DG** – Dark Green; **MB** – Matt black

▤ Blue
▥ Red
▧ Anti-chafe finish

Linear
Miniature
All a/c will eve
" Explosive Canopy"

EMERGENCY RELEASE
EXPLOSIVE CANOPY
BREAK GLASS PULL
HANDLE TO EXTENT
OF CABLE THEN TUG

LH Side View depicts
Trainer a/c cockpit

Upper I.F.F. Antenna

Pitot-static probe

UHF/TACAN Antenna

Titanium mu

Port elevation ▶

DSG
DG
DSG
DSG
DG
DSG
DG

Wing pivot area
DG
Upper Spring finger seals – 9 per side
DSG
Frangible panel
DG
Upper cooling air inlet
Windscreen Was

Tailderon pivot flexible fairing

Pitot probe
DSG
DG

Orange & black [×4]
DG
DSG

Passive ECM Antenna

RH Side Vie

DG
DSG

Double slotted flaps – 4 per side. All operate simultaneously. An interlock prevents deployment at wing-sweep angles greater than 25°

DG

Leading edge slats – 3 per side. All operate simultaneously. Not deployed at high wing sweep angles

DSG

Spoilers – 2 per side. Left & right operate symmetrically for "Lift Dump" or differentially for roll control. at wing sweep angles less than 45°

DG

Note: Wing sweep angles are fully variable between 25° and 67° and wings sweep symmetrically!

DSG

Wing Tip Obstruction Light LH Red , RH Green

MB

▲ Plan view
Starboard wing extended

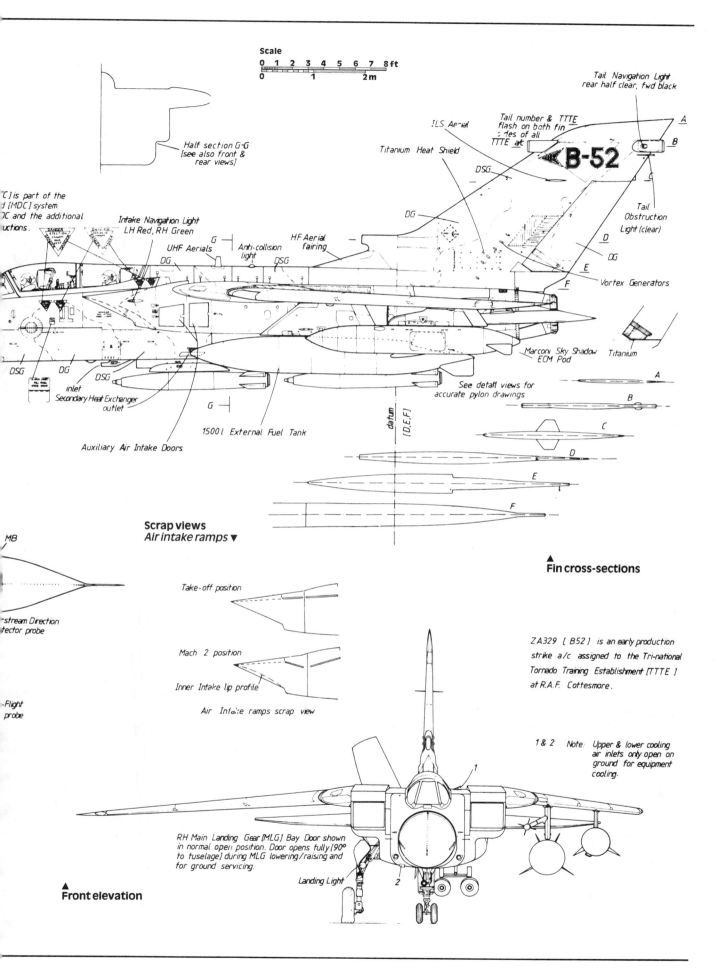

Scale

0 1 2 3 4 5 6 7 8 ft

0 1 2m

Half section G-G
[see also front &
rear views]

Tail Navigation Light
rear half clear, fwd black

Tail number & TTTE
flash on both fin
sides of all
TTTE a/c

ILS Aerial

Titanium Heat Shield

DSG

B-52

'C) is part of the
[MDC] system.
DC and the additional
uctions.

DG

Intake Navigation Light
LH Red, RH Green

UHF Aerials

Anti-collision
light

G

HF Aerial
fairing

DSG

DG

DG

Tail
Obstruction
Light (clear)

D

E

Vortex Generators

F

DSG

DG

DSG

inlet
Secondary Heat Exchanger
outlet

G

1500 l External Fuel Tank

Auxiliary Air Intake Doors

datum
[D,E,F]

See detail views for
accurate pylon drawings

Marconi Sky Shadow
ECM Pod

Titanium

A

B

C

D

E

F

Scrap views
Air intake ramps ▼

▲ Fin cross-sections

MB

stream Direction
tector probe

-Flight
probe

Take-off position

Mach 2 position

Inner Intake lip profile

Air Intake ramps scrap view

ZA329 [B52] is an early production
strike a/c assigned to the Tri-national
Tornado Training Establishment [TTTE]
at R.A.F. Cottesmore.

1 & 2   Note: Upper & lower cooling
air inlets only open on
ground for equipment
cooling.

RH Main Landing Gear [MLG] Bay Door shown
in normal open position. Door opens fully [90°
to fuselage] during MLG lowering/raising and
for ground servicing.

Landing Light

1

2

▲ Front elevation

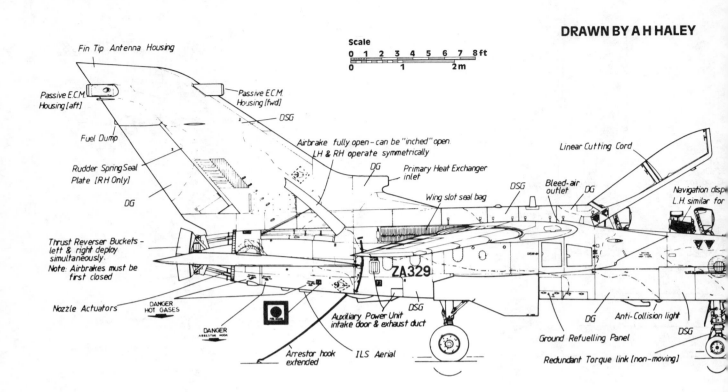

Fin Tip Antenna Housing

Passive E.C.M. Housing [aft]

Passive E.C.M. Housing [fwd]

DSG

Fuel Dump

Airbrake fully open – can be "inched" open. LH & RH operate symmetrically

Linear Cutting Cord

Rudder Spring Seal Plate [R H Only]

DG

Primary Heat Exchanger inlet

DSG

Bleed-air outlet

DG

Navigation disp[lay] L.H. similar for

Wing slot seal bag

Thrust Reverser Buckets – left & right deploy simultaneously. Note: Airbrakes must be first closed

Nozzle Actuators

DANGER HOT GASES

DANGER ARRESTOR HOOK

ZA329

DSG

DG

Anti-Collision light

Ground Refuelling Panel

DSG

Auxiliary Power Unit intake door & exhaust duct

Redundant Torque link [non-moving]

Arrestor hook extended

ILS Aerial

Scale

0 1 2 3 4 5 6 7 8 ft

0   1   2 m

A November 1981 photo showing GR Mk 1s from the Tornado Weapons Conversion Unit (TWCU) lined up at RAF Honington.
▼

▲
Starboard elevation

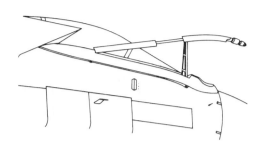

Colour notes
Air intake interiors – DSG; antennas – white or straw colour; walkway markings and most stencilling – MB; arrester hook – light grey; anti-chafe paint, early machines – light grey, later machines – dark grey; anti-collision lights have red lenses; fin tip – DSG with MB leading edge; HF antenna – DG with MB leading edge; danger triangles – red and white; fire access (6 off) – red and white; 'Danger hot gases' and 'Danger arrester hook' – red; rescue instructions – black on yellow; radome – semi-gloss black; anti-glare panel – MB; probes – natural metal; wing slot seal bag – medium brown textile; hot gases 'diamond' – red broken line and arrows, black divergent lines; taileron range of movement markings – red.

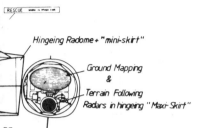

Hingeing Radome + "mini-skirt"

Ground Mapping
&
Terrain Following
Radars in hingeing "Maxi-Skirt"

DG

...rge amount of oleo
...ies with load, a/c
...n sweep angle etc.

▲ **Scrap view**
In-flight refuelling probe (not to scale)

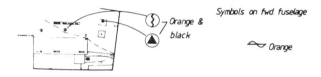

Orange &
black

Symbols on fwd. fuselage

Orange

▲ **Scrap view**
Thrust reverser bucket mechanism

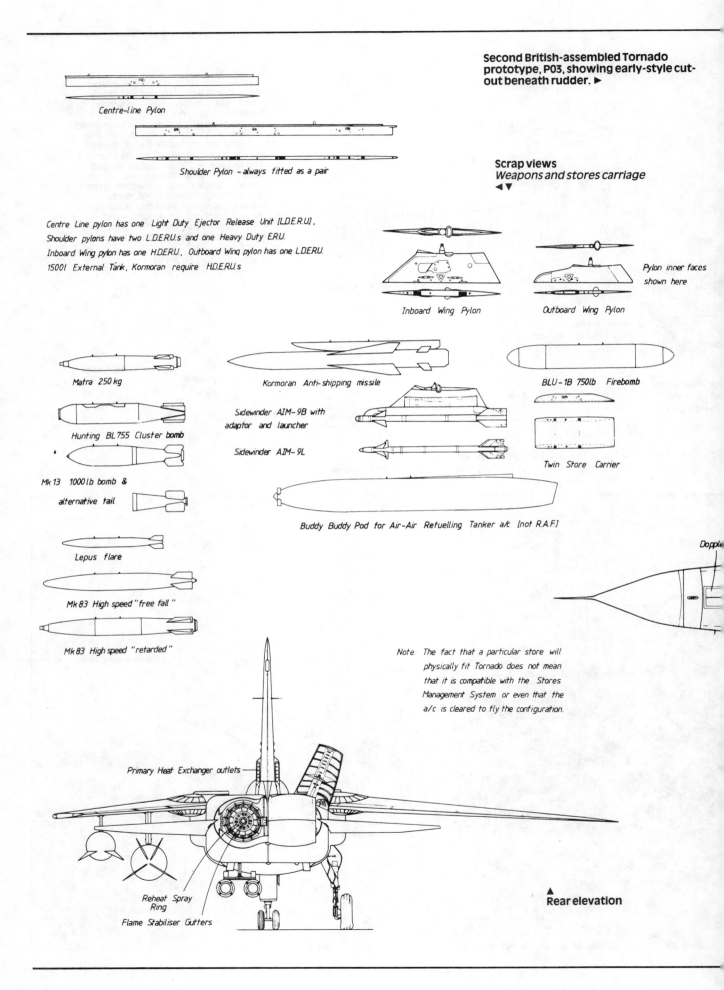

Centre-line Pylon

Shoulder Pylon - always fitted as a pair

Second British-assembled Tornado
prototype, P03, showing early-style cut-
out beneath rudder. ▶

Scrap views
Weapons and stores carriage
◀▼

Centre Line pylon has one Light Duty Ejector Release Unit (L.D.E.R.U.),
Shoulder pylons have two L.D.E.R.U.s and one Heavy Duty E.R.U.
Inboard Wing pylon has one H.D.E.R.U., Outboard Wing pylon has one L.D.E.R.U.
1500l External Tank, Kormoran require H.D.E.R.U.s

Inboard Wing Pylon

Outboard Wing Pylon

Pylon inner faces
shown here

Matra 250 kg

Kormoran Anti-shipping missile

BLU-1B 750lb Firebomb

Hunting BL755 Cluster *bomb*

Sidewinder AIM-9B with
adaptor and launcher

Sidewinder AIM-9L

Twin Store Carrier

Mk 13 1000 lb bomb &
alternative tail

Buddy Buddy Pod for Air-Air Refuelling Tanker a/c [not R.A.F.]

Lepus flare

Dopple

Mk 83 High speed "free fall"

Mk 83 High speed "retarded"

Note. The fact that a particular store will
physically fit Tornado does not mean
that it is compatible with the Stores
Management System or even that the
a/c is cleared to fly the configuration.

Primary Heat Exchanger outlets

Reheat Spray
Ring

Flame Stabiliser Gutters

▲
Rear elevation

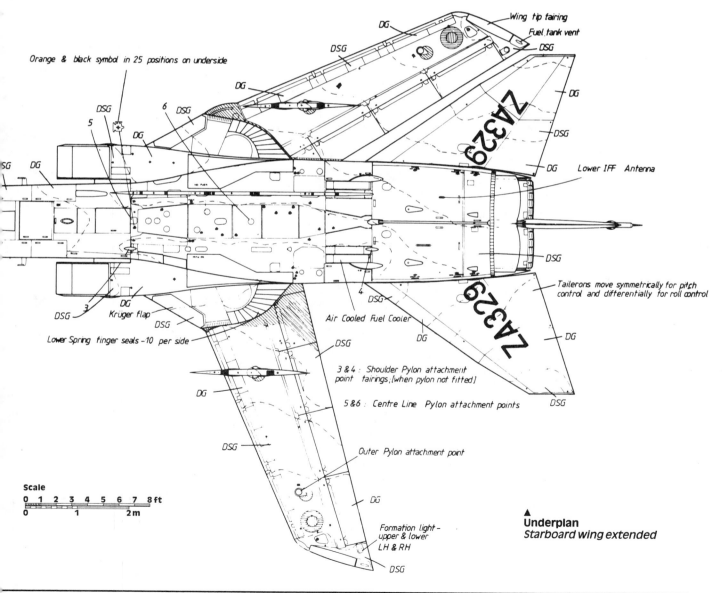

Orange & black symbol in 25 positions on underside

DG

DSG

DG

DSG

Wing tip fairing
Fuel tank vent

DSG

DG

DSG

DG

DSG

DG

ZA329

Lower IFF Antenna

DSG

6

DSG

5

DG

DSG

DG

SG

DG

ZA329

Tailerons move symmetrically for pitch
control and differentially for roll control

DG

DSG

3

DG

DSG

Krüger flap

DSG

Air Cooled Fuel Cooler

4

DSG

DG

Lower Spring finger seals -10 per side

DSG

DG

3 & 4 : Shoulder Pylon attachment
point fairings;[when pylon not fitted]

5 & 6 : Centre Line Pylon attachment points

DG

DSG

DG

DSG

DG

Outer Pylon attachment point

DSG

DG

Scale

0 1 2 3 4 5 6 7 8 ft

0   1   2 m

Formation light -
upper & lower
LH & RH

▲ **Underplan**
Starboard wing extended

DSG

The Publisher wishes to thank the following draughtsmen whose drawings appear in this volume

ARTHUR BENTLEY   A H HALEY

D H COOKSEY   E TAGE LARSEN

GEORGE COX   PAT LLOYD

GEORGE CULL   C J NICHOLS

J R ENOCH   IAN STAIR